Permission to Prosper

Permission

to

Prosper

What Working Wives Crave
from Their Husbands—
And How to Get It

Azriela Jaffe

PRIMA PUBLISHING

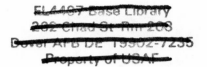

Copyright © 2002 by Azriela Jaffe

Published by Prima Publishing, Roseville, California. Member of the Crown Publishing Group, a division of Random House, Inc., New York.

PRIMA PUBLISHING and colophon are trademarks of Random House, Inc., registered with the United States Patent and Trademark Office.

Library of Congress Cataloging-in-Publication Data
Jaffe, Azriela.
    Permission to prosper : what working wives crave from their husbands—and how to get it / Azriela Jaffe.
        p.   cm.
    Includes index.
    ISBN 0-7615-6356-3
    1. Dual-career families. 2. Marriage. 3. Married women—Employment.
    I. Title.
HQ734 .J332 2002
306.872—dc21   2002071472

02 03 04 05 QQ 10 9 8 7 6 5 4 3 2 1
Printed in the United States of America

First Edition

Visit us online at www.primapublishing.com

This book is dedicated to my husband, Stephen, with whom I share a vision of creating an abundant life for our family and of becoming benefactors to our community. I know, honey, that you have absolutely no problem with my becoming a multimillionaire so that you can retire and spend your days gardening, learning, teaching, and getting to the hundreds of items on your to-do list. I'm working on it! I have more than your permission to prosper. I have your blessing. Thank you! I love you.

Contents

Foreword

I OFTEN GET asked to read an author's book and write its foreword, and almost as often, I refuse. It's not that I'm not honored or flattered by the invitations or that the books aren't important contributions; it's just that I'm too plain busy. In addition to my demanding clinical practice, a hectic on-the-road speaking schedule, and my own exhaustive writing responsibilities, I have a family who is more important to me than any of the above. So, I really shouldn't have accepted this invitation. And yet I felt compelled to say yes. But why?

Maybe it was because *Permission to Prosper* is a well-written, accessible couples book that focuses on relationship problem solving, and as a therapist who has devoted my life to helping couples save their marriages, that's right up my alley. But then many of the other books I had read fit that criterion. So that wasn't it. Maybe I was thinking about the many couples in my practice who had been struggling with the problems tackled in this book and envisioning how the well-thought-out solutions could help them. But that still wouldn't have been enough pull.

And then I figured it out. I had the painful realization that had this book been around several decades ago, it would have saved my parents' marriage. Although I was a young adult—seventeen and leaving for college—my mother ending her twenty-three-year marriage to my father was one of the most painful experiences of my life. It's still with me today as I near my fiftieth birthday.

What makes me so certain that this book could have made such a difference in the course of my mother's and, hence, my life? Although my mother's unhappiness in her marriage had several sources, a primary reason that she saw no other alternative but to leave my father was the differences in their perspectives about what my mother should do with her life. It was the late sixties, and like so many other women at that time, her "Leave It to Beaver" lifestyle left her feeling empty, as if something had been missing.

She decided to quench her thirst for meaning and connectedness to the adult world by suggesting to my father that she start a career. Being from the Old World and a traditionalist at heart, he would hear none of it. He was of the "A wife's place is in the home" ilk. At that time in our culture, he certainly was in good company—a fact that undoubtedly bolstered his position. Desperate for a way to feel happier, my mother persisted, a brave act for a woman back then—in her small circle of friends, she had no real role models of other women who had stayed the course and gone on to have it all.

Eventually, she managed to get my father to begrudgingly agree: "Fine, do what you want. But things at home better not suffer." My mother made some halfhearted attempts to find her place in the working world but always felt tremendous pressure to be mother/wife first and foremost, with no real understanding, compassion, or support from my father.

My father's reaction to my mother's search for happiness led her to believe that he didn't love her and couldn't love her. Otherwise, how could he have responded so self-centeredly to her attempts to find her way? Angry and resentful, my mother withdrew more and more. After months of contemplation, she came to the crossroads she had long been avoiding: "Either I stay in this marriage and die an emotional death, or I leave and truly begin to live."

One of the reasons for my great sadness about my parents' divorce is that I know it was avoidable. My father isn't a controlling, selfish man by any means. He was a product of the times when women were wives/mothers/housekeepers and men were breadwinners. He loved my mother and felt threatened by the emotional uprising inside her. He was scared that she wouldn't be there for him and for his children. He was worried about her forging into uncharted territory. His world was being turned upside-down. But rather than express his fears directly, he gave her admonishments and ultimatums.

Because my mother was dealing with her own unanswered questions, uncertainties, and feelings of discontent, she was not able to read between the lines. All she saw was his apparent need to hold her hostage, a perspective that prompted in her an even more intense desire to sever the marriage.

That's where this wonderful book comes in. Had my mother been given the acknowledgment for which she so desperately yearned, insights about my father's unreasonable clinginess, along with effective suggestions for approaching my father and the challenges they faced, her life might not have been distilled down to "either/or"; it might have been "both."

So, thank God for this book. Even though we've come a long way since the sixties, and millions and millions of women are now working women, many men still struggle with this fact. In addition, many women still sorely lack the tools to deal effectively with their husbands' "unfair" and "unrealistic" expectations. Infuriated, exasperated, and hurt, women often vacillate from caving in and resenting it to forging ahead bullishly without regard for their husbands' feelings. Both extremes are a formula for marital disaster.

This book provides alternatives. It's a practical book that will guide and inspire you not to give up your goals when the going gets tough in your marriage, but instead to find loving ways to have it all. It will help you achieve your dreams, to succeed, prosper, and grow. But unlike self-help books for women that offer advice on achieving personal goals without regard for the fallout it might have on relationships, this book is different. Azriela Jaffe understands how important loving, committed relationships are for women. She knows that many women, even highly successful, high-powered careerwomen, often measure themselves not by their salaries, titles, or professional achievements but by their success in love. Research tells us that married women are healthier, happier, and financially better off and even live longer. Choosing professional success over having a healthy, loving marriage is an incredibly shortsighted decision. And most of all, it's an unnecessary one.

If you have been mystified by the struggles in your marriage and your career, you've come to the right place. Once you read *Permission to Prosper* and put its sane advice into action, you will realize that it is possible to have it all. You will discover insightful ways to achieve your dreams without sacrificing the wonderful things your relationship has to offer. In fact, this book will help you transform your husband into the devoted fan and team player you deserve.

—MICHELE WEINER-DAVIS,
author of *Divorce Busting*

Acknowledgments

M ANY MEN and women participated in my research, through conversation, completion of my online survey, and letters in response to columns I wrote on this topic or my postings about this book. Because of the sensitive nature of this material, and because a good three-quarters of the research participants required confidentiality, we elected to share only first names in the book and in some cases to disguise the names completely. This book was shaped by your contributions, and I thank you for being willing to disclose thoughts of such a personal nature.

Thank you to loyal fans and readers of my ten other books and weekly newsletters. I know some of you bought this book just because I wrote it, whether or not the subject rang bells with you. I appreciate you every day, and I will continue to work hard to provide you with the excellence you demand from me.

Thank you to Elaine Pofeldt, editor of the Fortune Small Business Web site, who hired me to write a regular column, "Balancing Act," for the site where the idea for this book was spawned.

Jennifer Basye Sanders, editor extraordinaire, brilliant book packager, and, I'm honored to say, friend. We said for years that we'd work together. We finally did it. Let's do it again soon! You're the best.

Hashem: The best material I ever write comes from you. I am only a channel for your wisdom.

Much love to my husband, Stephen, and my three children, Sarah, Elana, and Elijah. They are my best reason for getting up in the morning, even when I went to sleep at 2 A.M. the night before because I was busy writing when the house got quiet!

Introduction: How This Book Came to Be

I F YOU are reading this book to learn how to be independent, you can put it down now. Single people are independent; they eat what and when they choose, have an entire bed to themselves, and answer to no one but friends, a boss, and perhaps a dog. If you are married, your course is no longer yours to chart alone, which is both the wonder and the burden of marriage—especially if you are a working wife. I have the following quote from Rebbe Menachem Mendel Schneerson framed on my bedroom wall. It inspires me to remember the vision of what a good marriage can feel like and why most of us marry.

> Love is not the overwhelming, blinding emotion we find in the world of fiction. Real love is an emotion that intensifies throughout life. It is the small, everyday acts of being together that make love flourish. It is sharing and caring and respecting one another. It is building a life together, a family and a home. As two lives unite to form one, over time, there is a point where each partner feels a part of the other, where each partner can no longer visualize life without the other at his or her side.

I am, thank God, a prosperous, successful, and powerful woman. None of that happened while I was single. All the best parts of my life developed while I was married. *Because* I was married!

In the spring of 2000, a woman I've never met accused me of setting the women's movement back twenty years by professing my ideas on marriage. Little old me, sitting in front of this computer. I never imagined I had such power. The same individual also suggested in not-so-nice language that I should do the world a favor and refrain from ever writing another word again.

The controversy that spawned this book began when I wrote three simple words in my then weekly column, "Balancing Act," for Fortune Small Business online. I addressed the subject of a working wife whose disgruntled husband was troubled that his wife made more money than he did. The FSB editor reported that the following few paragraphs from that column resulted in more mail than any other column since the inception of the FSB Web site.

Here are the precise words I wrote that created such a stir:

Behind many successful business women are supportive husbands who offer emotional support, help with child rearing, and, most important, permission to succeed.

Permission to succeed? Such an expression will raise the ire of the feminists of the world. Why should a woman need her husband's permission to succeed? Because if she doesn't receive it, implicitly or explicitly, she might sabotage her success. Many entrepreneurial women fear needing to choose between their marriage and a successful business.

When a man cannot or will not support his wife's entrepreneurial aspirations, it is usually because he is scared. He's scared that she'll leave him if she doesn't need his money anymore, or that he's less of a man if he's not even earning as much as his wife, or that she won't be around to take care of him anymore. His fear comes across as resentment and lack of cooperation. She can't understand why he isn't happy with more money pouring into the household. She doesn't think it's fair, because she always supported his career goals. Many wives don't understand this basic principle that applies to many men.

Who knew that these words would ignite such a firestorm? About one-third of the mail, from men and women, could be characterized as "Right on—thank you for saying what you did!" The other two-thirds of the mail expressed fury and disdain for my thoughts. Because I am a woman, I was viewed by many as a betrayer to the cause for women's equal rights.

At FSB's request, I went on to write a follow-up column, trying to defend myself and to vociferously argue my point. The furor made me wonder: Why do men and women have such trouble integrating a wife's career harmoniously into a marriage?

Here is a small sample of the angry letters I received from the original FSB article. They may help you understand why this issue touched a nerve.

From Sofia:

My first reaction to your article "Wives with Big Paychecks" was anger and disgust. I don't classify myself as a "feminist," but I am becoming more and more aware of the inequality issues women face today, the same problems that have quietly plagued the female sex for hundreds of years. It both infuriates and saddens me that women like you are only helping to keep us in this struggle.

In your article you wrote that women should ask their husbands for permission to succeed. Does the man own the woman? Should he have some kind of power over her? By asking his permission to succeed, the woman is placing herself below her husband. It is up to her whether or not she will succeed professionally—it has nothing to do with her husband. These are ideas from the Stone Age! Are you worth as much as a human being as your husband? I ask you to ponder that question.

Okay, I did. The answer is yes. My worth as a human being has not been lowered by my decision to involve my husband in decisions about my work life; it has been increased! From Bernice:

If you ask for your husband's permission, he might say no. Then what? I would never allow my husband to stop me nor boost up his ego by asking him. He is not my father; he is my partner!

Exactly. True partners do not make independent decisions; they make interdependent decisions. As Robert Schwebel, Ph.D., author of *Who's on Top, Who's on Bottom*, writes, "If you want to get exactly what you want every time, if you want to stay in charge of everything, then you shouldn't be in a relationship. You should be single."

From Elvira:

> Give me a break! The fact that I have succeeded in my pursuits would not cause me to obtain a condescending nod from my spouse. If he has problems with my success, he needs to look at himself, and not expect me to become subservient to his immaturity.

Yes, he needs to look in the mirror, but so do you. It is not condescending to you as a married woman to make career decisions with your marriage and family in mind. It is condescending to your husband to suggest that he is being immature if he expresses concerns about how your work life will affect him.

To prosper, a woman needs her own permission more than anyone else's. If she is married to an unsupportive or ambivalent man, she might hold herself back for fear of ruining her marriage. Other women may think, "The hell with him. If he can't handle it, too bad." But I offer another strategy. A woman can communicate with her husband in a self-respecting way so that she can gain his acceptance and approval. She may never hear the words "I give you permission to prosper, dear," but her husband's actions will communicate an implicit acceptance and even celebration of her success.

I am not suggesting that you literally ask your husband for his permission to prosper. I intend to teach you how to gain your husband's buy-in and lower his resistance to the issues in marriage that your work creates. You may be furious that women might even consider pandering to men or getting some Neanderthal's permission to succeed. If so, is your anger working for you? You might rant that my ideas weaken women, but they do just the opposite. You can gripe about men, or you can learn to live well with the man you have.

If your husband needs some reassurance to handle your success, and you want to be married to him and be successful, you have three choices:

1. Have an unhappy husband—too bad for him.
2. Sabotage your success so you don't lose your marriage.
3. Find ways to lessen your husband's grumpiness and fear so that you don't have to sacrifice your career for your marriage.

You don't need my help with numbers one and two; this book will show you how to make choice number three work for you.

Last but not least, from Natalie:

> Your comments are so offensive I can barely even begin to express my thoughts. This doesn't just anger feminists; it should anger everyone. May I suggest that you carefully study women's history and think about what it meant to our society when women were nothing more than their husbands' property? I hope that your husband continues to let you succeed, but if he doesn't, I hope that keeps you from printing such terrible advice. I will certainly never spend my money on anything you have penned.

Oh, well, looks like I lost a customer. By the way, my husband doesn't "let" me succeed. He celebrates, endorses, and encourages me, and he makes sacrifices to support my career. And I do the same for him. In a healthy, loving marriage with two partners who respect each other, each checks in with the other before making any major decision affecting the marriage.

However, Natalie's suggestion to look at women's history is a good one. A century ago, women couldn't vote, become educated, or work in a profession outside of their homes. When they did work off the farm, it was mind-numbing, tedious, sweaty factory work. They risked their lives to give birth, and they devoted their days and nights to their husbands and children.

My mother was an elementary school teacher. In fact, almost all of the working mothers back then were teachers or nurses. The joke was that you went to college for your teaching or nursing degree, but you were really going for your "Mrs." degree. Often, the women of that generation stopped working once they met "Mr. Right," or, like my mom, they worked in a family-friendly career with mothers' hours.

It was the wife's unquestioned responsibility to care for the family while the husband devoted his full attention and energy to earning a living. When I grew up, I saw little of my entrepreneur father—and this was normal. Nowadays it's not so fashionable for Dad to be absent from home for most of his children's early lives.

Yes, women have come a long way. Today the majority of college students are women. Virtually every career is now accessible to both men and women, even though some careers remain classically male-dominated. One-third of all businesses are started by women, and in a third of all marriages the wife earns more than her husband does. Only one out of five households still has only one wage earner, compared with two-thirds in the 1950s.

The glass ceiling still bangs many a good woman on the head. There is much progress still to be made toward equal pay and opportunity in the higher echelons of America. We're not where we want to be—complete access and equality at work—but compared with the lives of our mothers and grandmothers, we're moving at lightning speed. It could be better, but at the same time it's never been better for working wives—at work.

Unfortunately, the situation often isn't so rosy at home. Two-thirds of all divorces are initiated by women, and the correlation between (and, some believe, causation of) the skyrocketing divorce rate (over 50 percent) and women's financial independence is well-documented. A woman now has the power to walk out of a bad marriage. She has permission to prosper on her own instead of needing a man to take care of her. If her "needs aren't being met" and she's disappointed in her mate, there's better than a one out of two chance that the marriage will disintegrate. She is more likely now to have started a career before even having married, and since the average life span has increased from fifty years to nearly eighty, a marriage has to be a lot stronger to last a lifetime.

Many of us don't marry for a lifetime anymore. We want to live with our spouse only as long as it continues to feel good. If we don't like the way he acts, we'll upgrade to a better model. If the second marriage turns out not to be much better than the first, we are hopeful that the third time will do the trick. I am married to a man who divorced after many years of marriage and married me in his forties. Believe me, I'm all in favor of divorce and remarriage in certain circumstances, but regrettably, we've taken easy access to divorce to the extreme.

The Judeo-Christian bible contains a beautiful metaphor: Adam and Eve, formed by God as one flesh and separated only after they had started off as one combined human being. Now we women have become so committed to our independence that we no longer know how to be "one" with our husbands. We have radically changed our orientation toward work, but we're not so certain what we want from our marriages.

Working wives can't figure out why their husbands haven't yet gotten with the program. These men know it's not politically correct to admit their ambivalence or pain about their wives' careers, so they profess support—but then complain when dinner isn't on the table. They say, "Sure, honey, go for that promotion! I'm behind you all the way." And then, "Wait a minute. What do you mean I can't play golf on Saturday because I have to watch the kids?"

Women may declare their financial independence from their husbands, but many still crave being taken care of financially—and they are ashamed of this fantasy. Most women want full access to any profession they might choose. But a fair number of us, though we hate to admit it, want our pursuit of that profession to be optional.

We want to say, "I don't really have to work, because my husband takes such good care of our family. I *choose* to work, because it gives my life greater meaning and joy."

Cheryl, a woman who shared with me her struggles to accept marrying a high school–educated laborer who adored her, treated her like gold, but couldn't provide for her financially without help, admits:

> I came to believe that among all the other ephemeral beliefs that society places upon women, one of the strongest is to find and

marry the rich doctor and live happily ever after. We all want to have an easy life; many of us fantasize about not having to work (which is a different thing altogether from choosing to work). We stubbornly hope that money, prestige, and a life of entitlement will naturally beget happiness, much the same way we once insisted we had to have only name-brand clothing to be accepted in high school.

Women want full empowerment, as in freedom of choice and lack of discrimination. But lest we start whining about how slow the men have been to accept their new role as equal partner, we must acknowledge that our mixed messages are confusing our husbands. We still want our husbands to provide for us, even when we can provide for ourselves. We want our husbands to change and not change at the same time. No wonder they are confused and angry. So are we.

Let me ask you this: Is your fury and frustration with men getting you what you want? Are you happy in your marriage? Will your marriage last? Is yelling, complaining, whining, and giving your husband the silent treatment bringing you nearer to a close, intimate marriage and a thriving career? Do you really think it's just a matter of waiting for the men to catch up to our new, clearly superior way of conducting a marriage? In five years, or even ten, do you think that the proportion of men (now 8 percent) who take care of children full-time while their wives earn the family income will double, or even triple? How much change can a marriage absorb without straining from the pressure? In too many marriages, men and women are fighting more, loving less, and feeling perpetually dissatisfied. Working wives and dual-career marriages are here to stay. We have to figure out a way to take care of our marriage while—not instead of—nurturing a career.

William Doherty, author of the insightful and provocative book *Take Back Your Marriage,* teaches:

> People turn a critical eye on their marriage and spouse because their mate is a poor marital service provider and they fear that the original purchase was a mistake. Our consumer culture teaches that we are all entitled to an exciting marriage and great sex life and if we don't get both, we are deprived. The consumer attitude turns marital disappointments into marital tragedies and constructive efforts for improvement into entitled demands for change. We speak of personal desires as if they are constitutional rights.

We are often so obsessed with personal freedom and entitlement that it's no wonder the concept of permission to prosper generates an emotional reaction. But do married people have the right to choose, with no obstacles or considerations, how they will live life? We'll discuss the answer to this question in chapter 1.

I assure you, nothing I will say in this book is antithetical to a woman's ability to create an empowered, meaningful, intimate life full of choices and opportunities. The question is this: How do we achieve a level playing field at the office without leveling (i.e., destroying) our marriages in the process? Men need our compassion, forgiveness, and commitment. We need to teach them how to support us in the ways we need. We must also return the favor. We must work this out together, with our spouses. Our children are depending on it. And so are our businesses and careers.

A husband's support makes a huge difference in a woman's career. A working wife with a supportive husband is like a rocket ship. Her husband is filled with pride and joy. He is her safe place to land as well as her launch pad. She can soar without him—maybe even in spite of him—but *with* him is definitely better.

Traditional wisdom says, "When Mama's happy, everyone is happy. When Mama ain't happy, no one is happy." That might be true, but I'd add, "When Papa ain't happy, Mama ain't happy, so if we want Mama to be happy, we've gotta figure out a way to help Papa feel happy, too." In a close, loving marriage, Mama won't relish her happiness if what she's doing to get happy makes Papa unhappy.

Chuck was one of the many men who completed my research survey (yes, it wasn't only women who responded!) with this simple suggestion, repeated by countless others who responded to my questions. If you are married to a man who is suffering anxiety about your career commitments, Chuck insists, "Dump the insecure gentleman and get yourself a real man."

> If my wife made more money than me, I'd rejoice! I'd slaughter the fatted calf, buy a new car, and enjoy replacing shoes more often than every three years.
>
> —William

Ah, and exactly what is a real man? He'll eat quiche, rub your shoulders when they hurt, high-five you when you make your first million, and take the kids for the weekend so that you can go away with the girls to the spa. Sounds good. But there are lots of "real men" who don't fit this description, and they are still decent, loving husbands and fathers.

Do you know what saddened me the most about the multitude of surveys returned to me? The number of men and women who repeated this sentiment: "If your husband can't handle your career, he's a jerk. Leave him and find someone better."

If you are married to a verbally, physically, or sexually abusive husband, do not ask for his permission to prosper. Get help, and get out of that marriage. But if, like most of us, you are married to a true mortal—a man who carries love for you in his heart, right alongside his fears, insecurities, frustrations, and at times selfish attitudes—there is plenty you can do besides leave him. You can radically transform your marriage from a source of tension to a haven of support. It's not as hard as you think.

A Note from the Author

THE PERMISSION-TO-PROSPER principles are *not* designed to help working wives learn to live with an abusive, controlling husband. If your husband engages in any of the following behaviors, I urge you to seek counseling from professionals who are trained in helping abused women:

- He physically hits you, or threatens to, even once.
- He rapes you when he wants sex and you don't.
- He regularly attacks you with insults, character assassination, and self-esteem-destroying language.
- He tries to stop you from having a life outside of your marriage—your own friends, your own money, your own schedule, your own possessions.
- He treats you like his slave or employee, with him as the master.
- He is a drinking alcoholic, drug user, active sex addict, or gambler who is not willing to seek treatment for his addiction.
- He is involved in risky, lawbreaking activities.
- He is having an affair, or multiple affairs, and he won't end those relationships and work on reviving a committed, loving marriage with you.

We differentiate in this book between (a) improving a marriage worth saving by taking responsibility for your part in creating tension and (b) releasing unwarranted guilt and responsibility that you have taken from an abusive man. You do *not* need permission to prosper from a man who is not your loving, respectful partner in life. You need to give yourself permission to leave any man who is making you unsafe.

If you are married to a decent guy but your marriage isn't all you hope for, join the crowd, and read on.

CHAPTER ONE

The Permission-to-Prosper Philosophy

What It Is and Is Not

M ANY PEOPLE, men and women alike, have a strong re-action to the title of this book. You may be offended that a wife would ask (or need) her husband's permission to suc-ceed, or you may be thinking, "Well, *of course* wives need their husbands' consent to succeed. Duh!" Whatever your opinion at this moment, you may be surprised at the power and sub-tleties inherent in the notion of "permission."

Every word in the title—*Permission to Prosper: What Work-ing Wives Crave from Their Husbands and How to Get It*—was carefully chosen; changing even one word would drastically alter the philosophy.

We're going to examine what each of these words means: Permission, Prosper, Working Wives, and Crave.

We'll start with the loaded word first: Permission.

Permission

WHAT EXACTLY does "permission" mean, and why does it offend so many people? Let's start with the dictionary definition: Permission—"the act of permitting"; permit—"to allow, consent, tolerate, authorize, and indulge, to give opportunity for." The confusion and controversy generated by a woman's attempts to balance career and family obligations was apparent in the March 2002 issue of *Redbook* magazine. The magazine featured a lengthy article about a well-known movie actress who is also a wife and the mother of three children. Running alongside the article was a lovely picture of the actress curled up with her two preteen girls. The caption read, "People say, 'You've worked so hard for this. How can you turn down a big movie?' I look at the kids and I think, How can I not?"

So it's considered noble to turn down work for the sake of the kids. Let's applaud the actress's commitment to putting her family first. But would it be considered noble, or just plain foolish, if she turned down a movie role because her absence was making her husband grumble? Apparently, it is suspect if a woman compromises her desires to take care of her husband's needs, but if she alters her own desires for the children's sake, she is acting as any good mother would.

Is a married woman entitled to her husband's unconditional love and support for whatever urges, desires, and cravings she has in life? Of course not! Nor is a husband entitled to his wife's unquestioning loyalty and support for every whim he entertains. What if one partner verbally abuses the other day in and day out? Is that person still entitled to unconditional love? No—we'd all agree. Men and women, husbands and wives, have a right to stand up and say, "I can't live with this. Something has to change. This is hurting me."

Your marriage and home are a place where you hope to let your defenses down and be wholly accepted, even the darker, shadowy parts of yourself. You hope that you won't be abandoned for becoming ill, for going through postpartum depression, for dyeing your hair bright red by mistake, or for being imperfect in all kinds of ways.

Over the long years of your marriage, you hope to be loved so deeply that you never doubt your spouse's commitment and adoration; there's no place you'd rather be than your marriage, and being married to your spouse helps you become the finest human you can be.

Receiving love in a marriage comes from giving love and from behaving in ways that are respectful of your partner's wishes. If a husband is entitled to set limits and boundaries to behavior that is painful to him in his marriage, then it follows that in his role of husband, he should be involved in decisions related to his wife's career, especially if her work triggers an emotional response in him.

In the same issue of *Redbook,* a nationally known couples expert counseled a woman who worried about her husband's displeasure with the demands of her career and her resulting absence from the household. This was the misguided advice: "You have a right to the career path you want. If he's going to be a part of your life, he must support your goals, just as you support his."

Where is the wife's entitlement to her husband's emotional support for her career written in the marriage contract? Does he know that he agreed to this? Do his feelings factor at all into her career decisions, or is this a case of "Too bad, jerk—grow up. I'm going to do what I want, because I'm a grown-up and you can't tell me what to do"?

If spouses focused more on their obligations to each other and less on their individual entitlements, they would have much stronger marriages. If a wife expects her husband to be at her side as a steady partner for the rest of her life, she is obliged to treat him with respect and to honor the truth of her commitment to her work. It isn't only about her; it's about him, too.

Working Wives

NOW LET'S examine the phrase "working wives" in the title. This is critical. The whole concept of permission to prosper does not apply to single women. They can do whatever they want to do. Why does marrying change all that? Shouldn't a woman keep her rights to personal freedom when she marries? What is this, Afghanistan?

Here's what I believe about marriage: Once you marry, there is almost no decision that is completely yours to make anymore, just as your husband should consider your needs and wishes before making decisions of his own. It's advisable to discuss before marriage what you and your prospective husband believe about marriage, decision making, career choices, parenting, finances, and all the other complicated issues married partners must deal with. In earlier decades, wives and husbands assumed that men would make the major decisions and earn the family's living and that women would care for the home, raise the children, and nurture their husbands. This assumption changed drastically over time, particularly in the aftermath of World War II. Often, the women who had entered the factories to fill in for absent men were something less than ecstatic about returning to the kitchen afterward.

Regardless of your initial perceptions about marriage, when you shift from living your life as an *I* to a *we*, everything changes. There are millions of people who fight this idea—and look at the divorce rate. Two individuals who marry but live together as two *I*s, worshipping their independent rights and freedoms, don't have a marriage—they have a living arrangement to lower expenses, share a few meals, get regular sex, and raise children. Being married in your heart and soul changes the way you make decisions.

> Real giving is when we give to our spouses what's important to them, whether we understand it, like it, agree with it, or not.
>
> —Michele Weiner-Davis,
> *Divorce Busting*

Most people would expect that some decisions in a marriage are always mutual, like where to live, what religious practices to engage in, how to educate children, even what car to buy. I wrote the book *Two Jews Can Still Be a Mixed Marriage: Reconciling the Differences Regarding Judaism in Your Marriage* to acknowledge that a married couple might engage in different religious practices within the home even if both are "Jewish." One might keep kosher outside of the home and the other not. One might attend synagogue every week, the other only on the high holidays. But still, they are deciding together where and how to be different. The approach recognizes that this is the couple's issue, not just two individual spiritual journeys that happen to clash.

At what point does the expectation of joint decision making in a marriage break down? Aren't you entitled to some semblance of independence even if you marry? Yes, some—but probably less than you think.

You are no more entitled to your husband's unconditional support of every career choice than he is to your support of his. If he wants to invest your life savings into playing options on the stock market, is chasing a promotion that will take him away from you and the kids for two weeks a month, or is missing dinner four nights out of five because his boss is dumping work all over him and he doesn't know how to say no, it's not just his business; it's your business, too. Permission to prosper runs in both directions. If you want the right to have input into decisions your husband makes about the work/family balance, he deserves the same from you.

Let's say that you abhor going to the dentist. You're so scared, you put off getting your teeth cleaned and examined until the pain in your mouth is unbearable. You have the right to decide if and when you are going to go to the dentist—it's your mouth, right?

But what if your procrastination resulted in several thousand dollars' worth of dental work because you neglected small problems until they grew into larger ones? What if a regular lack of cleaning your teeth gave you a bad case of morning breath? Now you'd be hard-pressed to argue that your decision to avoid the dentist was about only you and not your spouse. Your spouse would have to deal with bad breath and a big drain on your joint checking account because of your choices.

What if you chose to ignore a lump in your breast? Your decision to make? I suppose, theoretically—if you were single. But as a mother and a wife, aren't you at all morally obliged to find the courage to face this calamity, to spare your husband and children the grief of your death if at all possible?

What about what you choose to eat every day? Okay, drinking either Coke or Pepsi is an individual decision. (There are a few of them left.) But what if you are a good fifty pounds overweight, don't want sex anymore because you hate your body, and are in danger of becoming diabetic? Still entitled to your decision to stuff your face with a dozen doughnuts for lunch because you are stressed at the office?

In theory, you have this right, but what it means to be married is that you think like a *we*, not an *I*, and you make decisions accordingly. You go to the dentist or the gynecologist, even when you're scared.

In a committed marriage, if you want true, lifelong intimacy with your husband, you must surrender the *I* to the *we;* the *I* will not always get its way, but the benefits of *we* are worth the effort. When you are married, what you do for a living and how you do it are indeed your spouse's business, and therefore he's entitled to his full range of feelings and requests—even if sometimes what you say to him is "No!" He still has the right to ask.

When my original column on this topic ran on Fortune Small Business online, the argument that dozens of people shouted at me could be summarized this way: "He'd never ask for her permission for anything related to his career, so why should she ask him for permission to succeed?"

If the assumption in this accusation were correct, the permission-to-prosper ideology should die a quiet death. But permission to prosper is not about the husband's right to control his wife; it is about the expectation of involvement in the life choices of your spouse, male or female. Women and men in close, intimate marriages understand immediately what I mean by permission to prosper. They regularly include each other in any work-related decision either of them wishes to consider.

Don't you often crave the close, intimate marriage you dreamed of on your wedding day? We all do. Although each marriage is unique, you can create one of three different kinds of marriage. (And some will have a marriage that is a blend of more than one.) The theme of gaining and rejecting permission is prominent in all three of these marriages. However, only one of them provides an environment that nurtures deep, spiritual, stable bonding between two individuals over a lifetime. As you read these descriptions, see which one resonates with your experience of marriage.

CONTROL-CENTERED MARRIAGE

These are two *I*'s who strongly resist becoming a *we*. Their marriage is characterized by constant power struggles, fighting, and a pervasive feeling of win/lose. The so-called winner of each fight doesn't always feel much like a winner, but still the goal is to win his or her way. Permission issues are self-serving and feel like emotional blackmail: "Do what I say or else I won't love you, have sex with you, stay married to you, etc." These spouses view each other as obstacles in the way of getting what they want rather than the means to get what they want. Mutual respect is absent; the two lovers have become competitors.

Some control-centered marriages are characterized by feisty spouses who take turns bossing each other around.

Other marriages cast one spouse in the controlling role and the other in the submissive role. If a woman should land in the submissive role, she might dream of a more equal partnership, but either she didn't pick a man capable of it or she chooses to be dominated for a host of complex psychological reasons. Some women do find it easier to leave decisions (and responsibility) in the hands of their husbands. Unfortunately, if the day dawns when they want more of a voice in their marriage, they may find it's too late.

Consider Debbie. Because she's married to a man with a temper, she has chosen to surrender to him on just about every decision in the household. But she has her way of controlling him, too. This is not a marriage with much intimacy, which probably explains some of her anger. Debbie asks me with some heat, "How could you suggest that a woman ask her husband for permission to do anything? That's what my husband expects of me, like I'm his little woman and he's the Mafia or something, ruling the roost. Well, let me tell you something. He thinks he's got me totally under his thumb, but he's the fool, because I found myself another man who treats me decently. I won't leave my husband, because of the kids, but he isn't controlling me like he thinks he is."

Don't worry, Debbie; there's no room for a control freak in the permission-to-prosper philosophy. Abusive behavior is never rationalized or endorsed. Having an affair might seem like sweet revenge, but you are attempting to control your husband as much as he is controlling you. Your weapon is just a bit sneakier. Each of you is concerned with your own personal gratification rather than with respecting the other. But it doesn't have to be that way. Even in a marriage that seems stripped of all intimacy, couples can find their way back to true caring for each other.

FAIRNESS-CENTERED MARRIAGE

We're still talking about two *I*s not becoming a *we*, but the difference between this marriage and the control-centered marriage is that these couples take pride in their equality, fairness, and politeness. The chores are divided equally; enormous attention is paid to keeping score of who has done what and whose turn it is to get time off for good behavior. Permission flows constantly between these partners, but it's always about making a trade—you can do this if I can do that.

> When egos lock horns, nothing else matters. There is no rational explanation for the hideous way two adults treat each other once they start into the dominate-or-destroy mode.
>
> —Fred Hartley,
> *Men and Marriage*

On the surface, this marriage looks loving, even ideal. Equal partners, right? But don't let it fool you. It's still an *I*-centered marriage. The true focus is on making sure that I'm getting my needs met and that my spouse isn't getting more than his fair share of anything that should be coming to me instead.

Individuals in this kind of marriage overuse the words "should" and "shouldn't." They have personal standards for the way a marriage "should" operate, and if something might improve their relationship but doesn't seem "fair," they'll refuse to do it.

Michele Weiner-Davis gives this example of what a husband in a fairness-centered marriage might think: "Yeah, I know calling her when I'm out with my buddies and telling her when I'll be home works to make her less mad, but I don't think I should have to do that!" Here are a few more examples of the ways couples "should" on each other:

- "I shouldn't have to cook a meal every night of the week—what does he think I am, his maid?"
- "I shouldn't have to apologize to her for our fight when it was her fault in the first place!"
- "I shouldn't have to keep the bathroom clean to her standards when she's such a perfectionist!"
- "My spouse should give the kids a bath tonight—I did it last night!"
- "My spouse should be home for dinner—it's the only time we have together as a family!"
- "My spouse should be available for sex more often—does she want me to start looking elsewhere? I'm not a monk!"

In a fairness-centered marriage, permission is all tied up with what each spouse believes is fair; permission is withheld if there is a perception of inequity. How do you know if you are in a fairness-centered marriage? Take a look at how much score keeping is going on. Do you expect something in return every time you do a so-called favor for your spouse? Do you have a pervasive feeling that "my spouse owes me because I did something nice for him"? Do you expect your spouse to behave toward you as your mother and father did toward each other when you were growing up?

Julia and Robert's marriage is a classic example. They keep a written log of chore expectations, time spent on various household responsibilities, and even how often they have sex. They've worked out a trade that suits each of them: If Julia has sex with Robert three times a week or more, it's only "fair" that she gets something she wants.

"I don't have the sex drive my husband does," Julia says, "and after ten years of marriage, we stopped pretending that I would, or could, so we came up with something else that seemed fair to both of us. I really like to sleep in on the weekends, but I'm in charge of the kids most of the time. Robert agreed to take care of the kids at breakfast if he got 'it' the night before. Seems like a fair trade to me!"

Julia and Robert might have a solution that works for both of them. Fairness negotiations can be quite effective. But if a couple starts keeping score for everything from child care to sex, the marriage may feel more like a business partnership, or two siblings sharing an apartment, than an intimate relationship. You don't have to trade intimacy for equality. You can have both at the same time. You just have to learn how.

GOODWILL-CENTERED MARRIAGE

This is the ideal we are shooting for, even if we aren't always certain how to achieve it. The first two forms of marriage are acceptable working partnerships, but the kind of lifelong romance that makes you still glow when your husband of forty years walks into the room—that's the stuff that comes from a very different kind of marriage, one far too few of us have seen or experienced. Why? Because we're so darn scared of giving up control.

In a goodwill-centered marriage, an expression I first learned from bestselling couples expert Susan Page, two *I*'s became a *we*, and ironically both *I*'s are getting their deepest individual needs met; this marriage is a true haven of support and security. The focus is on supporting each other rather than "getting my own way." Each partner is willing to give to the other, to put aside his own needs from time to time, and each gets great joy from doing so. This couple doesn't understand why I have to write a whole book on the notion of permission to prosper. For them, mutual give-and-take and cooperation on any decision that could affect the other is a basic expectation, even an obligation, of marriage.

> When you defer to another person because you choose to, don't label it as being a doormat, because you wanted to do that. Assertiveness does not mean that you always get your way, but that you feel really good about the choices you made.
>
> —Stanlee Phelps and Nancy Austin, *The Assertive Woman*

In a goodwill-centered marriage, each spouse is often stretching to accommodate the other, maybe even changing some aspect of herself to make her spouse more comfortable. However, she fundamentally feels accepted by her spouse for who she is, and criticism, nagging, and disdainful judgment are largely absent. Because constant negativity isn't there to eradicate their loving feelings for each other, they are more easily able to extend themselves to each other, even when it means giving instead of getting. They are motivated by feelings of love and a genuine desire for the other person to get the very best life has to offer.

This couple isn't embarrassed about being dependent on each other—they are proud of it. Their biggest fear is not losing their own way—but losing each other to death or disability.

A goodwill-centered marriage has lots of appreciation, gratitude, compliments, respect, pride in each other, and trust flowing through it. It feels good to be in a marriage like this. *Permission to prosper is not about entitlement and control; it is about mutual respect.*

Kathy and David are the epitome of the goodwill-centered marriage. Kathy shares her gratitude for the fundamental way that David's love has inspired her tremendous success in the business world:

> I believe that without David's unconditional love, I would not be what and who I am today. I have a confidence level that I never expected was possible. I am so sure of myself and confident that I can always speak my truth. It does not matter to me if people don't like me—I have all the approval I need at home. His support of me allows me to take risks and not be afraid to fail, because I can always go home. Honestly, David is the most important person to me in the world. I can live without my family, possibly my friends, but he makes life worth living for me.

■ ■ ■

So, AFTER looking at these different kinds of marriages, and thinking about where yours fits in, how does the word "permission" grab you? If you are in a control-centered marriage, it may disgust you that anyone thinks you need it (even when you do). If you are in a fairness-centered marriage, you are most likely obsessed with making sure you are giving and getting the same amount of permission from each other. If you are in a goodwill-centered marriage, permission is a natural expectation that comes from your accepted interdependence. If you discover that you overemphasize control or fairness in your marriage, this book will provide you with alternatives that will help bring you and your husband joy and peace.

Crave

MY PUBLISHER initially suggested changing the subtitle of this book to *What Working Wives Need from Their Husbands,* and I panicked. What's the difference between "need" and "crave"? Light-years. The women who get angry at me for expressing this philosophy don't read the title carefully. They think that I am saying "need," and that's part of what triggers their rage. They want to know, "How dare you suggest that a woman needs a man's permission to succeed?"

They are right. Women don't *need* men to approve of them, permit them, direct them, or shape their lives. Women are entirely capable of running their own lives. All of us, men and women alike, are struggling to grow out of societal expectations that we must look, act, and behave in prescribed ways in order to be "good enough."

Depending on our childhood and how well our self-esteem was nurtured, we bring into our marriages varying degrees of terror regarding abandonment and lack of approval. Some women are so self-assured that they need little ego stroking from their husbands. Other women are deeply hurt if their spouses are critical; their husbands may complain that their wives seem to be a bottomless pit, that no expressed appreciation is enough to fill that hole.

Jim Warner, author of *Aspirations of Greatness,* teaches:

> As adults, our subconscious comes to believe that others will love us only if we perform to their high standards. We conclude

that no achievement is ever good enough, and there's always the threat that someone else will do it better. As a result we become performers, pleasers, and victims whose identity and worth depend on the affirmation of others—parents, boss, spouse, coworkers. Without a natural grounding of self-worth, we feel under constant scrutiny to see if we measure up. Our playfulness and self-love go into shadow.

As we leave our parents' home, where approval seeking was the task of childhood, it is natural that we transfer that psychological hunger into our marriages, where we yearn for the elusive feeling of unconditional love and acceptance that we didn't get at home. The craving a woman has for adoration, respect, and approval by her husband is as natural to her as breathing.

But we must not make this mistake: Adoration, respect, and our husbands' approval are not essential to making a success of ourselves in the work world. Plenty of women with unsupportive husbands—or with no husbands at all—make it to the top, and they are damn good at what they do. What we are talking about here is a woman's hunger for acceptance and approval and the sense of well-being she feels in the world when that hunger is met.

Many women place their husbands in a double bind. They expect men to be sensitive and tender, able to express their feelings (as long as they're the right feelings, that is), yet strong enough to keep their wives safe and secure. When we are honest with ourselves, we women often have two cravings that seem mutually exclusive: We crave our husbands' approval and permission for us to prosper, and we also crave being provided for so that we don't *have* to prosper on our own. We'll address this conundrum in greater depth throughout the book.

Prosper

ON TO the last word in the title that needs explanation: Prosper. Again, we rely on Webster's for the official definition: "to succeed, thrive, and grow in a vigorous way, prosperous condition; good fortune, wealth and success."

Every husband wants his wife to succeed. The question is, in what? Maybe he wants his wife to be a fabulous lover, a gourmet cook, an entertaining hostess to his friends, an enjoyable companion on the golf course, or a terrific mother to his children. Many men want their wives to succeed in work-related pursuits as well. But even the man who genuinely wants only to be married to a homemaker is not a guy who doesn't want his wife to succeed; his criteria for success may be measured by how well she cares for him and the children.

Wives don't crave only their husbands' permission to succeed. They crave permission to *prosper*, which is a level beyond succeeding. To prosper might mean she makes more money than he does or she makes enough money to be financially independent of him. To prosper may mean he has to deal with his fears of the sexy hunk with a BMW who works with her. To prosper might mean she grows personally and spiritually and starts asking—even demanding—changes in their marriage to support her internal growth. To prosper could mean she becomes a desirable, powerful, self-assured woman, and he has to face his own insecurities about being good enough for her. If his wife prospers in a "vigorous way," he might be asked to pick up the slack at home. To endorse his wife's success is relatively easy. To endorse his wife's prosperity is a whole lot more courageous, loving, and generous.

One night I was discussing these themes with my husband, Stephen, and I asked him, "Why don't you obsess about winning my approval, the way that I crave yours?" His answer: "I haven't worried about that since I married you!" Stephen was plenty focused on gaining my respect and overall hero worship while we were courting. As soon as he put that ring on my finger and we pledged a lifetime of love, his need for my approval lessened. He still wants to be respected, but he experiences himself as having met the test. He can relax in our marriage and focus most of his approval-seeking energies on his work, where the obsession for meeting with approval still occupies his mind a great deal.

So why do I continue to fret about receiving my husband's approval? Why is it so threatening when he is disappointed or angry with me? Why can't I let it roll off my back with a "who cares, that's his problem" attitude, the way he seems to do with me? Am I biologically programmed as a woman to crave my husband's adoration, no matter how long we're married, how often he tells me that he loves me, and how confident I am that we're together for life?

I have pondered these questions for many hours, and one night the answer dawned on me. Most men are obsessed with performance at work because they have been programmed by family and cultural influences to believe their survival depends on it. Since the beginning of humanity, if a man didn't perform at work (killing that night's dinner), he and his family went hungry. A man's self-worth is so closely tied to his work that if, at a social gathering, you ask a man to tell you something about himself, he'll usually start the conversation with "I'm a . . ." and then he'll tell you about his profession.

Ask a wife and mother that same question at a social gathering, and she'll often pull out pictures of her kids before telling you about her job. It's not that her career isn't important to her, because it is. If this were a business setting, she would respond much as a man would, with her resume first. But a woman's fundamental identity is more closely connected to her role as wife and mother than corporate executive, businesswoman, or employee, even if her career is vital to her.

Why do so many women obsess over gaining their husbands' approval and permission to prosper? Because since the beginning of humanity, women have been taught to believe that their safety comes from being taken care of by their husbands. What naturally follows is this: A wife's primary job description in life is to make sure her husband is happy so that she will not be abandoned.

Logic tells us that when we start earning money, our obsession with being provided for should lift, because we can now take care of ourselves. But for many women it doesn't work that way. Programmed deep into our souls is a craving to be connected to our husbands and families. If prospering in our careers might threaten the stability of that which makes us feel safest—a loving, intact, stable family life—we will continually crave the reassurance that our men are happy and consider our career aspirations in the context of how it will suit our husbands and children.

I know that some women find this perspective objectionable. Sounds demeaning, doesn't it, to suggest that a woman could still, after all of the advances in equal pay and women's rights we've witnessed over the past fifty years, be driven above all else by the urge for connection to her husband and children? Do women honestly believe that their husbands are going to take care of them or that they can't take decent care of themselves? Haven't we moved beyond that nonsense?

Thank God, no. Maybe if a woman's craving for her husband's approval and permission to prosper has not diminished relative to her income, it's not really about power and control at all. Even when she has the prerogative to leave, she usually still cleaves to her husband for emotional, if not financial, support. Adolescents claim they want total freedom, but what they really want and need is the right balance of structure and roots and enough leeway to extend themselves beyond the confines of their parents' rules and ideals for them.

Women bring the same longings to marriage. They want both freedom and obligation, independence and accountability, the absence of responsibility and the cherished feeling of a family's depending on them. When a woman chooses to pursue one of these states of being, without its opposite, she may regret what she did not experience in her life. She will often feel "out of balance."

The question is not how women can stop caring about what their husbands think and exert their independence. Look at where that attitude got us. An outrageous divorce rate, for one thing. The question we must answer is this: How can we women thrive in a career while still being committed to the traditional idea that our husbands and children are our top priorities and that whatever we do with our work life must be positive for the entire family, not just for us? The question doesn't pertain just to women: Husbands, too, often need to learn to better balance their family and work commitments. When both partners give and receive permission to prosper and the marriage is filled to the brim with mutual love and respect, that marriage is likely to be a source of pleasure and encouragement for both.

Do you have to give up your career goals in order to make your husband happy? Can you enjoy a satisfied husband, thriving kids, and a meaningful career all at the same time, or are you kidding yourself?

Yes, you can be a happily married wife and mother with a meaningful, prosperous career. The first step is to be unwilling to settle for anything less.

CHAPTER TWO

Fundamental Principles to Reduce Tension and Increase Intimacy in Your Dual-Career Marriage

M OST PEOPLE enter marriage with a host of unspoken, perhaps unrecognized beliefs and expectations about marriage, husbands, wives, and the ways things "ought to be." Whether you know it or not, your beliefs shape every interaction you have with your husband—and some of your beliefs may be hindering the development of the intimate working partnership you want to create. This chapter explores five false beliefs about relating to your husband that you, as a working wife, may have. We will see the negative consequences that result from those false beliefs and discover positive alternatives to relating to your husband.

The principles communicated in this chapter will be useful whether or not your husband is interested in working on your relationship. Two of my favorite marriage experts—Susan Page, author of *How One of You Can Bring the Two of You Together,* and Michele Weiner-Davis, author of *Divorce Busting*—have instilled renewed hope in women who long ago gave up on their marriages, thinking, "I've tried everything, and it's hopeless. He'll never change."

Given the vast repertoire of relationship strategies available, chances are that you really haven't tried *everything*. You've probably been repeating the same habits that don't work, instead of learning new strategies for developing the intimacy and support you desire in your marriage. As the twelve-step programs teach, insanity is doing the same thing over and over again and expecting different results.

Here are some smart alternatives to help husbands and wives traveling the path of learning to live with, support, and love each other.

> The length of a relationship is not necessarily correlated with how well people really know each other. Some twenty-five-year relationships that have stagnated are really one-year relationships repeated twenty-five times. The keys to growth and in-depth understanding are openness and attention, not time.
>
> —Eric Cohen, *You Owe Me*

False Belief 1: A husband's world does not revolve around his wife the way a wife's world revolves around her husband.

Negative Consequence of This Belief: If you believe that you are less important to your husband than he is to you, you may see his every action (or inaction) through the lens of "You don't care enough about me and the kids." You will be convinced that your husband's career and leisure time are his priorities and that you and the children are secondary. You and the children are probably what your husband treasures most in his life, but because he is unskilled at expressing his devotion in your preferred way, you may feel perpetually resentful and

> YOU CAN bring down any good marriage in two years by
> focusing on what you aren't getting and how your partner
> fails to live up to your expectations. Obsess about his defi-
> ciencies and what you are entitled to. Then either criticize him
> all the time or withdraw from him and complain about how
> empty your marriage is. Focus only on his deficiencies and
> blame everything on marrying the wrong partner. He will in
> turn give you even less and thereby help justify your leaving.
>
> —William J. Doherty, Ph.D., *Take Back Your Marriage*

lonely. This man, who courted you with roses and love notes
and pledged his undying love for you on your wedding day,
may now seem more concerned with his golf score and his
new promotion than your happiness. Human beings have an
amazing capacity to see exactly what they expect to see.

Most wives want to feel like the center of their husband's
universe. Perhaps you haven't felt that way in many years. You
may worry that maybe he doesn't really love you after all. You
may be furious because after all these years of picking up his
socks and cooking his dinner and making love to him, this guy
doesn't appear to wake up in the morning and ask himself,
"How can I make my wife happy today? What does she need
from me?"

This just isn't fair, especially if each morning, before you
ever think about yourself, you begin thinking about what your
husband and kids need.

Michael Obsatz, Ph.D., couple and family therapist
and associate professor of sociology at Macalester College in
St. Paul, Minnesota, believes that this pain in a woman's heart

might be one of the reasons she may try to get certain emotional needs met from her career. He notes:

> A lot of men are self-centered, acting as if the world revolves around them. A woman may pour herself into her work to get the appreciation she is not getting in her marriage. When the woman stops being her husband's satellite and starts becoming her own planet, and he's expected to be her satellite, he doesn't know how to do that role. He hasn't been trained to be someone's satellite—he's only been trained to be the planet.

Positive Relating Principle 1: Give your husband the benefit of the doubt; he does care about you, occasional appearances to the contrary. Sometimes you just have to know what to look for.

Instead of wandering through your marriage muttering, "I'll believe it when I see it," try saying, "I'll see it because I believe it." Yes, there are self-centered jerks who really don't give a hoot about their wives, other than as a vehicle for getting sex, a meal, and a babysitter. Most men, though, are kind and loving and would tell you, "Be patient with me—I'm trainable," if they knew how. Don't label your husband as an unromantic clod, he may just live down to your expectations of him.

I have learned over the years to see my husband's love and commitment because I believe it is there. He, in turn, has learned to be "more romantic," which means acting differently from what comes naturally to him. I am his planet, and he is mine, and we can choose to be satellites for each other.

A husband may not wake up in the morning and think immediately about what to cook his wife for breakfast, but he might be obsessed with his career because of the pressure to bring home the proverbial bacon for his family. In a good marriage, he feels very connected to and dependent upon his wife. This is why it terrifies him when she becomes distant, diverting her attention and energy away from him and into her career.

The irony is this: Women have the reputation of being the family-centered, deeply committed ones in the relationship, more devoted to caring for the needs of their men than men are to caring for them. But caring and commitment can take many different forms. When a marriage breaks up, it's often the man who falls apart, while the woman is surprisingly stable. Women may seem more concerned with pleasing their men, but they actually seem to survive better without them than men do without their wives. Women may be likelier than men to enter marriage with conditional commitment—I'll stick around as long as you love me the way I think you should.

Men are more fragile and vulnerable than we acknowledge, because their lives *do* center around their wives, and this means giving up control. His world centers on you, and he knows it. He wants you to know that it does, too.

In a truly healthy marriage, each partner matters deeply to the other; each has the power to hurt the other or to offer encouragement, generosity, and support. Each is vulnerable— and each is likely to resist a spouse's attempts at control. We've moved out of the dark ages, when the man was the head of the house and what he said went, period. But the societal pendulum has swung so far in the direction of egocentricity and taking care of one's own needs that we've lost the

THE NEW working wife is angry because all these years his career didn't miss a beat. The kids grew up, but she didn't get a gold watch. She decides to go into a career, and he has concerns, but she feels entitled. His whole life is going to change, and instead of her saying, "We're a team; let's navigate this thing together," she says, "Look, I've put up with your bullshit all these years, and so now you're going to do this!" The whole transition starts off on a negative note. It could be a very positive thing for him—more money in the house, an interesting person to live with—but the benefits to him aren't communicated. What's communicated is her anger.

—From an interview with Michael Broder, Ph.D., a therapist

art of structuring our lives around a commitment for life to one human being for a shared journey that will require many self-sacrifices.

When you really get this about your husband, it will be far easier to feel compassion, instead of anger, when he exhibits an "unsupportive" attitude toward your career. Maybe he is just a selfish jerk. Or maybe he's lonely and scared silly, but he can't admit that. He may tell you that your business is a stupid idea or chastise you for not being home to put the kids to bed. He'll complain that the house isn't clean enough anymore or sulk about the good old days when you used to cook a meal. Anything but "I need you."

Your husband may express his devotion to you in a language different from the one you speak, but if you believe it, you just may see it. Take time to look for evidence that your husband's world centers on you. You may have to look at your marriage through his eyes, not your own, to see his truth.

False Belief 2: If I pamper my husband now, he'll expect it from me forever. He should just grow up and start acting like a man.

Negative Consequence of This Belief: When your baby is teething, you excuse her crankiness a little more readily, and you give her extra TLC. You might be up half the night rocking her to sleep, and although you aren't happy about it, you accept it as part of your responsibility as a mother. Eventually, the baby falls asleep in the comfort of your arms, and then you can get back to sleep—you hope!

Why do kids cry when they are teething? Because a new tooth is breaking through their tender gums, and it hurts. You know that this is for a good purpose, but all the baby knows is that it hurts. "Mommy, make the pain go away," she wails. You bring out the ice cubes, teething toys, and Children's Tylenol, and all of that helps, but still, it hurts. Eventually, the teeth come in, the pain vanishes, and the baby partakes in all of the yummy goodies on your table.

Why are we so forgiving and compassionate when our babies are hurting but so hard on our men when they are? Because we have an expectation that our grown-up husbands should be able to deal with their hurting in a more macho way, without being coddled by us as if they were babies. Sometimes we yell at them for hurting, when they really need a hug.

Change is difficult. No matter how wonderful your career and no matter how positive the long-term results for your marriage and family, the process of making changes can be painful for everyone concerned. Adopting a "get over it" attitude ignores the very real pain, confusion, and sense of loss your husband may be feeling. And he is unlikely to be supportive of your choices when it appears that you are unsupportive of his feelings.

You may feel that it's your time now—he had his. Or you might point out that you have entertained his clients and colleagues, and the least he can do in return is cook a meal for himself while you are entertaining yours. (Remember the fairness-centered marriage?) You may want to set the record straight once and for all—you are not his maid! The next time he complains about his dirty underwear piling up, you may be tempted to tell him where he can put his underwear.

Your husband may be feeling less significant and less important to you than he did before you took on your job. He listens to you talking about your career and your opportunities and wonders if he's lost your love and attention. Is he less important because you have a career now? The pain he is feeling is not politically correct for a modern, egalitarian male who wishes to support his working wife, so he may try to hide his feelings from you. Or he may look for evidence that his complaints are well-justified. Regardless of the way your husband expresses his confusion or pain, he needs to know that you understand and can give him time to adjust to change.

Positive Relating Principle 2: Recognize that your husband needs extra care and support from you during critical transition times—even when you are least inclined to give it.

What you view as unsupportive behavior from your husband might be evidence that he is not adjusting well to change. He may need extra attention from you for only a short time, until he gets his balance back. Still, you may fear that if you yield to his complaints, he'll ask for more and more until you have nothing left to give. You may worry that his dependence and demands will never end. Better, you think, to put your foot down now.

When a working wife's career changes, what she needs from her husband often conflicts with what he needs from her. What kinds of critical transition points affect a husband and wife in a dual-career marriage? Here are eight transitions that dual-career couples often face:

> People don't understand compassion. They confuse it with sympathy and with being a doormat. Compassion is the internal lubricant that protects human beings from each other's frailties.
>
> —George Pransky,
> *Divorce Is Not the Answer*

1. Moving from full-time mom to first job since the kids were born
2. Increasing work hours from part-time work to full-time career
3. Starting a business on your own
4. Starting a business with your husband, or working to support your family while your husband starts a business
5. Winning a promotion to a high-pressure job, or changing fields to a more demanding career
6. Balancing multiple, conflicting demands when both your career and your husband's career demand extraordinary energy and sacrifice at the same time
7. Being forced suddenly, and perhaps reluctantly, into the role of primary earner when your husband retires, becomes disabled, or is downsized

M Y HUSBAND and I are both lawyers. When he's work-ing on a brief, he expects the world to stop; nothing's more important than the case. When he comes up for air, he returns to being a decent father and husband again. Me? I'm expected to do my client work while never missing a dance recital, soccer game, or Saturday-night date with my husband and his clients and their wives. Does he think my work is less important than his just because he bills out at a higher rate? You know what I'd like for a Saturday-night date every once in a while? For my husband and kids to get out of the house so that I can work in peace and quiet!

—Joan

8. Becoming more prosperous than your husband while he is still working

During these critical transition times, the working wife is often exhausted and emotionally flattened. She needs a wife! Instead, she's coping with a needy husband who may seem to be just one more person who has to be taken care of. She wants him to grow up—fast—and learn how to take care of himself so that he can better care for her and help her with the incessant demands of child rearing and a career. She's furious that he can't (or won't) support her the way she needs.

When someone you love dies, everyone expects you to go through a mourning period as you cry, rage, and adjust to your loss. When you radically change your role in your home and marriage, your husband might experience a form of mourning. His previous way of life is dying, and though it may eventually be replaced by something even better, he will grieve his losses and lick his wounds while he gets his act together and learns how to support your new needs.

Throughout this book, we'll discuss how you can give your husband at least some of what he needs—even when you feel you have the least to give—in order to help him become your best supporter. Contrary to your fears, if you give him love and reassurance when he needs it, you won't have a dependent, resentful whiner the rest of your married life. It's when you push him away and lay claim to your "rights" and independence, just when he's feeling the most vulnerable, that you risk ending up with a self-centered, insensitive partner.

> The dominant view of marriage in today's America is less a partnership than a joint venture between two parties concerned with preserving their own autonomy.
>
> —William J. Doherty, *Take Back Your Marriage*

False Belief 3: I have to grab this career opportunity and run with it right now, or I may never have the chance again. My husband will just have to deal with it.

Negative Consequence of This Belief: We learned a great deal from witnessing the dot-com explosion—and its crash. Thousands of entrepreneurs got rich, but too many others went broke and lost their marriages and their perspective. An impulsive frenzy like this can wreck a marriage, especially when a working wife is seized by this fixation: "I have to go for it. This is my window of opportunity. It will never happen again!"

How can enthusiasm wreck a marriage? you may ask. Let's say a wife takes off like a rocket, turning her household

M Y FAITH has played a huge part in knowing and establishing my priorities. I could easily be more ambitious, but I cannot, in my heart, put my work ahead of my husband. I don't believe God would honor that decision. I know other women who also claim to have faith yet put their marriage on the back burner. I've recently written a book. My husband hates the time this book has taken me away from him; he also resents that there'll probably be no income for all my blood, sweat, and tears. To look for a publisher now would be disastrous for our marriage. I'm going to publish it after my husband retires in July of 2003, when he's got more emotional energy to deal with it.

—Shelley

upside-down and all but abandoning her husband and family. No surprise: He tries to slam the brakes on her career—not because he doesn't want to support her but because it's too fast for him or because he doesn't feel involved or needed in her life anymore. *It's the speed of her travels, not where she's going, that creates the friction.*

The woman in the box above understands that she's married to a supportive man, but he has his limits and she has pushed against them too hard with the added working hours devoted to writing a book.

Positive Relating Principle 3: Accept that the speed and devotion with which you approach your career should be a shared decision—and, yes, the same rule applies to him.

This statement probably makes some women nervous, even angry. Don't worry; I am not suggesting that a woman's career be ruled by her husband. I'm not telling you that if he says, "You're moving too fast for me," you should salute and snap to attention: "Aye, aye, sir. Tell me how fast I can move— you're the boss!"

I am suggesting this: If a husband decides to go after a new promotion that will require an additional twenty hours a week away from home, he should get his wife's buy-in first. She might be fine with it, but she should be asked whether she's up for the contribution she'll have to make in order for him to pull it off, and she should have some veto power if it's more than she can handle. In the same way, he should be given the same right when his wife wants to make changes that affect both of them.

If you are single, go ahead: Spend twenty hours a day working, sleep the other four hours, eat at your desk, have no life outside of work, and take pride in your complete devotion to your goal of becoming a multimillionaire before the age of thirty. Who cares how you spend your time?

But if you are married, any decision you make to spend an abnormal number of hours away from home, mentally or physically, is not yours to make alone—unless you want to ultimately end up alone. Moving at a speed you and your husband agree on, rather than racing along on your own, doesn't mean you are giving him the power to run your career. You are demonstrating that your marriage is at least as important to you as any income or fame you are chasing.

A recent moment in the kitchen with my son, Elijah, age four, illustrates the potential devastation of too much speed. Elijah and I were making homemade breadsticks for that evening's dinner. He'd donned his apron and was standing on the chair in front of the kitchen counter, helping me put the ingredients into the mixer. Finally, we were ready to begin the mixing. "Can I turn it on, Mommy?" he asked. I said, "Sure." (Like an idiot.)

Words can not adequately describe the mayhem that followed. Elijah flipped the mixer switch to a full ten (instead of level one, as suggested by the recipe), with seven cups of flour inside. Within three seconds, flour, yeast, sugar, eggs, and the rest of the mess was flying all over my kitchen, plastering Elijah and me and coating every square foot of us and the kitchen with "yuck."

It seemed like twenty minutes passed as I shrieked and struggled to turn off the mixer. By the time I reached the machine, the damage was done. Elijah just looked at me, stunned, with an expression somewhere between "Ain't I cool, Ma? Look what I did!" and "Am I in big trouble now?"

It took an hour to clean up the mess, long enough for me to realize how well this incident demonstrates why a new business or job for Mom can be a train wreck for a marriage. It's all about speed.

A gradual start gives everyone time to adjust and gives your husband time to learn new ways of stepping to the plate. A super-fast launch puts everyone into a tailspin—the woman who is now immersed in the world of work and its pressures and those family members trying to get used to her absence. Add lack of sleep and a high level of anxiety and loneliness in the house, and it's no wonder that a marriage can start to crumble under the pressure.

If you absolutely have to dash, make sure you have your husband's support. If you don't have his permission to prosper, read the rest of this book to see how you can gain it.

False Belief 4: If I stop trying to change my husband, I'll be stuck in an unsupportive marriage forever. Believe me, if I don't push him, he'll never change!

Negative Consequence of This Belief: Would you change just because your husband pushed and insisted? Probably not. Nor is your husband likely to say meekly, "Yes, dear," when you push and prod him. (And be honest: Would you respect him if he did?) You may wish you could order him around like an employee, but if your husband senses your attempts to control, change, or improve him, how much cooperation will you get?

Why should he rush to sign up for your hubby-improvement program? You've already got his weaknesses labeled, his deficiencies as a husband clearly defined, and a surefire plan to make him a more acceptable human being. Pushing him to change may cause him to dig in his heels more deeply than ever, out of sheer self-defense.

When all else fails, you may try to persuade him with your actions—withholding sex (or granting it if he gives you what you want), giving him the silent treatment, or catching him at an inopportune time and insisting that the issue be resolved right then and there. These strategies are unlikely to win his attention and commitment.

Positive Relating Principle 4: Give up trying to whip your husband into shape. Your appreciation and praise of him are far better motivators than insults or score keeping.

It has taken me ten years of marriage to finally "get" this one, and I am still imperfect in my ability to act on it. At least now I am aware of my old habits, and I pull myself out of them more quickly. I've finally learned that my husband will

A N OVERWHELMING percentage of "this bothers me, will you please change" dialogues end up unhappily— with arguments, resentments, self-consciousness, and guilt. Focus on dissatisfactions creates a negative tone that undermines and weakens a relationship. A negative tone makes it less likely that the other person will see and correct his or her mistakes. To facilitate change in people, treat them with understanding and goodwill so they will drop their armor and regain wisdom, creativity, humor, and compassion—assets that increase productivity and responsiveness.

—George Pransky, Ph.D., *Divorce Is Not the Answer*

never be "guilted" into changing anything substantial for me. The closest I'll come is a "Yes, dear," with lack of follow-up on his part because he didn't really mean it. He was only "yessing" me. My best approach is to raise the goodwill quotient in our marriage so that he genuinely wants to make me happy and will work with me to achieve that goal. As we learned earlier, to receive love and support, you must be willing to give love and support.

This book will teach you dozens of strategies for relating to your husband in a way that stimulates and inspires him to love you the way you yearn to be loved.

False Belief 5: My husband may be abusive, cruel, and selfish, but if I just stick it out long enough, he'll get better.

Negative Consequences of This Belief: I can't say this strongly enough: The permission-to-prosper principles are not designed to help you learn to live with an abusive, controlling man. If your husband engages in any of the following behaviors (which are also listed at the beginning of the book, but they certainly bear repeating), I urge you to seek counseling from professionals who are trained to help abused women leave their abusive partners and find safety.

- He physically hits you, or threatens to, even once.
- He rapes you when he wants sex and you don't.
- He regularly attacks you with insults, character assassination, and self-esteem-destroying language.
- He tries to stop you from having a life outside of your marriage—your own friends, your own money, your own schedule, your own possessions.
- He treats you like his slave or employee, with him as the master.
- He is a drinking alcoholic, drug user, active sex addict, or gambler who is not willing to seek treatment for his addiction.
- He is involved in risky, lawbreaking activities.
- He is having an affair, or multiple affairs, and he refuses to end those relationships and work on reviving a committed, loving marriage with you.

If you have been made to feel like a piece of trash in your marriage, you must not put up with more of the same. If you can check off one or more items on the list above, you don't need to read about how to please your man. His foul mood, destructive addictions, or errant way of life is not your fault or responsibility. The last thing you need to do is bend yourself like Gumby to please a man who is destroying your life.

Women need to stop apologizing for, and owning, problems they did not create. Still, not everything that upsets or frustrates you is "abuse." What is the difference?

Positive Relating Principle 5: Distinguish between being abused and feeling disappointed. Learn to tolerate disappointment and to trade entitlement for vulnerability.

Many times I've heard women say, "I can't tolerate my husband's lack of support anymore. I deserve better." Yes, you can tolerate it. You already are. You may not like it; you may believe that it is grossly unfair. You may look at your friends' husbands and think you got a raw deal and you could do better. ("Sally's husband cooks dinner three times a week and takes the kids to the park every Sunday so she can get her work done, while my husband comes home, grabs the remote control, and waits for dinner to arrive in front of him.") If you are married to a decent man who is disappointing you, this book will help you influence his behavior to be more helpful and loving, but first you must be willing to give your husband your full commitment—*before* he changes.

There is a difference between needs and wants. When you don't discern between what is absolutely essential to you in your marriage (freedom from abuse, basic respect and trust, a mutual willingness to work on improving your marriage, a solid commitment) and what is desirable, you may become grossly dissatisfied with your marriage. If you convince yourself that your husband should be more supportive, loving, and affectionate (and whatever other virtues your list contains) and that you cannot and should not tolerate the absence of these attributes, you may already be halfway out the door.

> L IVING IN a relationship where the commitment is tentative or intermittent is like living in a rented house. You don't like the color of the walls, but you don't want to put the time and money into painting them, because you may be in another house soon enough. It's just not worth the investment.
>
> —Susan Page, *Now That I'm Married,*
> *Why Isn't Everything Perfect?*

You and your spouse entered into your marriage with a host of expectations of each other, formed from your families of origin, your religious beliefs, your personalities and preferences, and the conversations you may have had during your courtship. Beyond the normal, more global expectations of fidelity and partnership in child rearing, the tension arises from the details.

Unconsciously, we translate hundreds of expectations into phrases such as "If you loved me, you would . . . (or you wouldn't)" or "If you could do that to me, you couldn't love me." These expectations can be large ("I expect you to provide for our family financially," or "I expect you to show respect to my mother every Sunday even though you can't stand her") or small ("I expect you to say 'I love you' every day before we leave for work in the morning"). The so-called small expectations may quickly escalate out of proportion because of the meaning you ascribe to them.

For example, my mother and father have gone to bed together, after watching the 10 P.M. news, virtually every night of their forty-plus years of marriage. They can probably count on two hands the exceptions due to illness or business travel. This kind of closeness, day in and out, is what I thought was normal for a married couple. My husband, however, grew up with a mother and father who went to bed separately, when each was tired.

So I took it personally when my husband went upstairs to sleep whenever he felt like it, rather than joined me in the intimacy of going to bed together. He thought it was weird to go to sleep on someone else's schedule. Over the years we've learned to give and take. The point is that my expectation that he would go to bed with me each night, just as my mom and dad do, was unreasonable and led me to be disappointed in him in the early years of our marriage.

Sometimes your spouse's expectations are crystal clear to him—and to you—and at other times, expectations are unconscious or unspoken. All too often, the offending partner doesn't even know she did something wrong—until her spouse gets upset, that is.

Often, the reason your expectations aren't being met is that you communicate them with an air of arrogance and entitlement that is a huge turnoff to your husband. If your attitude says, "You owe this to me because you are my husband," you are unlikely to meet with heartfelt cooperation.

The wife who believes she is entitled and who acts like a shrew poisons any possibility that her husband will respond to her with loving kindness. When she scolds her husband for not being good enough to her, he feels either hopeless about pleasing her or angry about being lambasted for his inadequacies. Neither emotional response will encourage him to make positive changes.

A woman's incessant need to shape her husband into her servant and ideal partner is not rooted merely in her desire for power and control. What's beneath that drive? One possibility is her vulnerability.

When a wife gives up trying to improve her husband, she feels two frightening, conflicting feelings. She fears he won't meet her needs unless she coerces him to do it, which means she'd be left alone to take care of herself. And what if she did allow herself to love her husband just the way he is? If she could stop trying to change him, she might discover that he is an amazing human being. Then, when faced with how much she loves him, she would have to live with her terror of losing him.

In my parents' generation, if you wanted a divorce, you'd better have been married to a man who was dangerous, who was completely unable to earn a living, or who was a lecher or a thief. Now if your husband doesn't turn you on anymore or you don't like his bathroom manners or he doesn't buy you flowers on Valentine's Day and he never says, "I love you," such disappointments are grounds for divorce and ripe feeding ground for a well-justified sexual affair.

> Your partner has a right to be sloppy or absentminded or workaholic or selfish. Personality characteristics might displease you, but he doesn't have to change them for you. You have a right to what you want, but so does your partner, so you won't end up with everything you want.
>
> —Susan Page,
> *If We're So in Love,*
> *Why Aren't We Happy?*

If you ever catch yourself thinking, "If only he'd change, our marriage would be perfect," just laugh at yourself. Nothing in marriage, or life, is that simple. If you are being abused, you need to make drastic changes—now. If you are merely disappointed, read on to discover ways you can effect positive change in your marriage.

To summarize, here are five anchor principles for relating to your husband more effectively:

Positive Relating Principle 1: Give your husband the benefit of the doubt; he does care about you, occasional appearances to the contrary. Sometimes you have to know what to look for.

Positive Relating Principle 2: Recognize that your husband needs extra care and support from you during critical transition times, even when you are least inclined to give it.

Positive Relating Principle 3: Accept that the speed and devotion with which you approach your career should be a shared decision—and yes, the same rule applies to him.

Positive Relating Principle 4: Give up trying to whip your husband into shape. Your appreciation and praise of him are far better motivators than insults or score keeping.

Positive Relating Principle 5: Distinguish between being abused and feeling disappointed. Learn to tolerate disappointment and to trade entitlement for vulnerability.

Let's see how these principles are applied.

CHAPTER THREE

Husband Resistance

What It Looks Like and What to Do About It

A WIFE CAN succeed without her husband's active support, but it's like hiking alone up a mountain with a backpack full of rocks. Wouldn't you rather picture yourself running a marathon while your husband cheers you on from the sidelines, handing you water bottles and snacks along the way and greeting you with a warm hug and a smile at the finish line?

Wives suffer when their husbands suffer. If a wife believes that her husband can't endorse her career success, she may unconsciously (or deliberately) sabotage her career, because even in this modern feminist age, most married women value marriage and family over all other aspects of their lives.

Let's take a closer look at what keeps husbands from being the cheering supporters their wives long for.

Your Husband Could Be Scared and Angry

IF YOUR husband is unsupportive of your career, he is probably scared, angry, or both. When a working wife changes the rules and tries to reshape well-established roles in the relationship, her husband has no choice but to change, too; if he doesn't welcome those changes with an open heart, his wife is likely to witness his resistance.

Men are far more complicated than the stereotypical, macho guy who needs only material success and lots of sex in order to be happy. Most men, including the one you're married to, are more vulnerable than you might think.

You always wanted a sensitive man? You probably have one. But instead of giving you back rubs and whispering adoring poetry in your ear, he may be having a tantrum. You don't always get "sensitive" on your terms.

Men are confused, and no wonder. They have every right to be scared and insecure. Women are divorcing their husbands at record rates. If their husbands don't measure up, there are better men at the office to choose from. Husbands are being asked to do more around the house and with the kids—but according to their wives' standards. A man has to get used to his wife not greeting him at the door when he comes home from work, except maybe to leave him with instructions on how to warm up dinner or where to pick up Johnny from soccer practice.

Wives who pursue a career do change the rules of marriage for their husbands, whether they intended to or not. In simpler times, men assumed that pleasing their wives involved a few simple actions: earn a good living, make her proud with your accomplishments, show up on important occasions like anniversaries and birthdays, remember her once in a while with a nice gift (especially jewelry), help her feel secure in the world and adored in the bedroom, and, when applicable, be a decent dad.

Now what's a man supposed to do to make his wife happy? Wash the dishes. Be her date for her company Christmas party and strike up a rapport with her boss. Listen to her vent about work—without solving her problems for her. Give her a hug when she's too tired to move, but don't take over responsibilities at home unless she asks you to. Learn to read her mind. (If she has to ask for it, it doesn't count.) If he really loved her, he would instinctively know what she needs.

Dual-career marriages pose other challenges to husbands, too. Our culture has encouraged men to measure their value by their salary and career achievements. It can feel highly threatening to a man to have a wife who's more successful than he is, especially if she outearns him. It can be difficult not to criticize and lash out at a wife whose accomplishments threaten his own.

> Men's hearts are tender and easily wounded, and often by the most surprising things.
>
> —Daphne Rose Kingma,
> *The Men We Never Knew*

Wives aren't responsible for every negative emotion their husbands feel, but it can certainly seem that way sometimes. We can take ownership of every negative emotion he has and feel compelled to fix his mood so that he feels better, so that we can feel better. But when your husband is happy and whistling around the house, do you give yourself any credit, unless it just happens to follow lovemaking or a fabulous meal?

Women have been absorbing the emotional moods of others since birth, beginning in our families of origin, where we craved our parents' and peers' approval above all else. Now married, we might crave our husbands' admiration. Many of us still carry the sorrow from those adolescent and young adult years, when we never felt good enough to please our moms or dads or to rate as popular among our schoolmates.

It is not surprising that a wife will go to great lengths to help her husband be happier, or at least not to introduce actions that will make him unhappy. If a wife believes that her career decisions could make her husband grumpy, she might feel that the only way to fix him—and therefore to make herself feel more at ease—is to remove the source of tension and curtail the career demands that are creating pressure. Before you leap to conclusions and do something rash, like quit a rewarding job or slow down your businesses, let's look first at what may be the real cause of your husband's negative mood. You might not have to do anything so drastic; just make a slight course correction.

So why does your husband seem scared and angry more often since your business started to really take off? Because he may not be sure he's good enough for you anymore. Because his sexual and emotional needs are not being met—but it's politically incorrect for him to complain about it. Because he may be terrified of being alone, even when he complains about not having enough space. Still, even if his feelings are understandable, what should you do to bring out his best?

Compassion and Smart Strategy Work Better Than Justified Anger

THIS BOOK easily could have been a male-bashing book. I could have filled its pages with whining, righteous indignation and railing speeches about how unfair it is that husbands treat working wives so poorly, how women still are not getting equal rights in marriage, and how they deserve better.

And where would that have landed you? Would you love your husband more? Would your marriage be more likely to last a lifetime? Would you get what you want—a supportive, helpful husband? I don't believe so. We could all have one big pity party and cry the blues about our victimhood, but this would only perpetuate and worsen the problem.

Yes, it's true, men often miss the mark and either refuse to give us wives the love and encouragement we crave or don't know how. We do often deserve better. But my aim is to help you get more of what you want, not to give you heaps of sympathy because you live with a guy who isn't ideal.

Own responsibility for your part in your marriage, especially if your relationship isn't what you want it to be. I am not suggesting that it's all your fault and that you are solely responsible for your man's moods. But you do play a significant role. Every relationship depends on the way two people communicate; your husband is reacting to you as much as to his own feelings. This is good news, actually, because you have complete control over the part of the problem that is yours, so you can fix it.

Let's take a look at five different ways that your husband might express his dissatisfaction or lack of support for your career commitments. Your husband might be the poster child for one of these, or he may alternate between two or three of them, depending on the circumstances. With each one, we'll offer a quick tip about what you can do to alleviate some of these symptoms.

1. The Passive-Aggressive Husband ("I know I said I'd help—sorry, I forgot.")

Let's start with a working wife's pet peeve. He says he'll do it—and then he doesn't. Unless you nag him, of course. Then he complains about your nagging. Even when you nag, he still might not do it unless he feels like it, on his own terms and according to his own schedule.

The most frustrating aspect of this pattern is that he says that he'll do it—whatever the "it" is. So, he "yesses" you, but he's not sincere. What he's telling you is "I don't want to deal with your anger for saying no, so I'll pretend that I'm going to do it by saying yes, but I have no intention of really doing it. Or if I ever do, it'll be my way, when I feel like it."

> Men can be brave when it comes to killing bugs, chasing a burglar, and millions of other manly things. But these usually brave souls can lose their nerve with women.
>
> —Daylle Deanna Schwartz,
> *All Men Are Jerks,*
> *Until Proven Otherwise*

The passive-aggressive pattern extends beyond the annoying yessing habit. It includes all your husband's Jekyll-and-Hyde tendencies, sometimes loving, supportive, and wonderful, and sometimes a selfish creep. You don't know where you stand with this guy. He sounds supportive, but then he breaks his promises. He gives lip service to the notion of equal parenting, then "forgets" to take your daughter to her orthodontic appointment.

This husband excels at apologies, which is rare for most husbands. But his apologies come with an agenda: "If I say I'm sorry, you have to excuse my behavior. The slate is wiped clean, and I'm in your good graces again." He expects that any disappointing behavior of his will be automatically forgiven by those magic words "I'm sorry."

We are accustomed to judging a person's attitude by his actions. This husband's inaction is just as eloquent. He is communicating plenty to you when he *doesn't* do something you want.

The more passive-aggressive a husband's behavior, the more badgering and shrewish his wife seems to become. This dynamic destroys romantic energy in the marriage.

Depending on a passive-aggressive husband's support is like trying to squeeze Jell-O. It is all the more frustrating because it appears as if he's right there with you. When he lets you down, you feel betrayed and confused. Is he on your side or not? Can he be trusted to keep his agreements?

Yes and no. The passive-aggressive husband is usually reluctant to initiate conflict by telling you how he really feels. He may be ashamed of his feelings, wanting to be a better husband to you, but he isn't ready or willing to follow through on his promises.

Until the two of you learn to communicate in a way that is not threatening for him, he is likely to continue this cowardly behavior. He cannot consistently be there for you, even if you need him, until he works out his ambivalence and you learn how to talk to him without nagging. If you are married to a guy who is passive-aggressive by nature, you will probably live with this behavior for your entire marriage. But it's a matter of degree. Choose to have realistic expectations, and lighten up a bit about the times he "forgets." (Sometimes, like you, he really may have forgotten!) The good news is that you can influence his behavior by your own.

One quick tip: My four-year-old son, Elijah, has developed a frustrating habit. When I scold him for bad behavior, he breaks out in a chorus of "I'm sorry. I'm really, really, really sorry!" He thinks this passionate apology will absolve him of all responsibility for his actions and, therefore, any punishment. I tell him, "Elijah, I'm glad you are sorry, but sorry isn't enough. You can't do this again." Then sometimes, despite the apology, he still has to experience the consequences of his behavior.

If your passive-aggressive husband lets you down and then apologizes, accept his apology, but let him know how he has disappointed or hurt you. Ask him respectfully for what you need from him in the future. A calm voice will encourage him to listen and take responsibility for his own behavior.

2. The Helpless Incompetent ("I'd love to help, honey, but I don't know how.")

He's happy to help you, he says, but he's not any good at it. The last time he took care of the baby, he left her in a poopy diaper until you came home two hours later because, he says, he doesn't know how to deal with "number two"; his idea of watching the kids is lying on the sofa and being available in case of emergency, because he claims that he falls asleep as soon as he tries to read your youngster a story, and of course it would be dangerous if the "babysitter" were sleeping. He says he'll share the cooking with you, but if he's in charge of dinner three nights a week, the best you'll see out of him is pizza or some other version of take-out. He knew how to cook just fine when he was a single guy living in an apartment, so what happened to his cooking skills? Did they wither from disuse?

You exhaust yourself after working hours to take care of all the household and family responsibilities that your incapable husband cannot, or will not, manage. You are furious with him for giving too little. What happened to the egalitarian marriage? What does he think this is, the fifties?

Your husband's apparent inability to care for the kids, do the laundry, or clean the kitchen beyond stacking the dirty dishes in the sink may be mind-boggling to you. What's so difficult about placing the dishes in the dishwasher, instead of in the sink? Are boiling noodles for spaghetti and opening a jar of sauce really too difficult for an MBA from Harvard? And what is so complicated about operating a washing machine?

Your husband's so-called incompetence derives from two things: a lack of training and skill, and rebellion. Sometimes he really *doesn't* know how to do what you find so effortless. Other times, he knows how but doesn't want to do it. He may feel that it is beneath him and that helping you with household work diminishes his standing as the head of the household. He may not do it because he doesn't feel like it. Or you may have set your requirements so high that he is discouraged from trying; after all, he never does it "right."

There are two kinds of helpless incompetents. Some men have been that way all their lives, and they won't change

> I was in the shower when my husband asked, "What should I feed Lily for lunch?" "That's up to you," I replied. "Why don't you pretend I'm not home?" A few minutes later, my cell phone rang. It was my husband saying, "Yeah, hi, honey. Uh . . . what should I feed Lily for lunch?"
>
> —Julie Ball,
> *Reader's Digest,*
> March 2002

without a serious reason (divorce or infrequent sex because of your building resentment). Then there are the guys who sincerely want to share the load, but because they are truly disabled or unskilled (or you won't let them do it their way instead of yours), they fail at the effort.

At his worst, the helpless incompetent gives up any ambition of his own and becomes what some working wives describe as a "mooch." Maybe he was downsized or fired. His business might have gone bankrupt. Perhaps he's too sick or depressed to work. This guy has given up his ambitions and responsibility and has turned breadwinning and caregiving over entirely to his wife.

One quick tip: You'll waste a lot of energy and possibly destroy your marriage by fighting over dryer lint and dirty socks if you are married to a guy who simply won't help you with kids and housework. If you believe that you will never change this aspect of your beloved and you want to remain married to him for other redeeming reasons, get household and parenting help by other means. Don't waste time and energy on a litany of "It's not fair!" complaints that lead nowhere but marital hell. If you are married to a truly incompetent, overwhelmed, gently resistant but well-meaning soul who needs training and loving encouragement, there is plenty you can do to improve your situation. We'll explore the details in chapter 8.

3. The Guilter ("Honey, I know you have to work tonight, but the baby misses you, and so do I!")

This guy knows all the buttons to push. He pouts about how lonely he is at night when you aren't home with him. He tells you often how much the children are missing you or makes sure you know that you missed Sammy's first steps. He reminisces about the good old days, when you used to cook more elaborate meals or when he grew up with a mother who was always home when he came home from school. He senses your ambivalence about working and your sadness at missing out on more time with your children and wishing you could be intimate more often with your husband. He has a way of frequently reminding you of your ambivalence.

This husband isn't a shouter, and anger isn't the medium through which he expresses his displeasure with your career. He is almost always polite, the Rock of Gibraltar for you, and your friends envy you for having married such a catch. He does do dishes, and he regularly pitches in with raising the kids. He truly wants you to succeed, and he makes a concerted effort to support your choices. Looking around at some of your friends' husbands, you feel you have no right to complain about your beloved.

Still, things could be better. You wonder sometimes if you are just too sensitive, but it annoys you when he makes sarcastic comments about how spaghetti and salad *again* is probably healthier than eating meat and potatoes, or he teases you about becoming a drill sergeant at home, just like at work. If he's angry with you, why doesn't he just tell you what's on his mind? It would be easier for you if the next time you called from the office to say you've got to work late, he'd get mad or tell you that he needs you to come home. Instead, he says in a sweet voice, "Gee, honey, that's too bad. I rented us a movie, and I was looking forward to cuddling with you on the sofa. I'm going to be lonely without you here."

You aren't likely to complain to your girlfriends about this guy, because he is "so supportive" of your work—at least on the surface. You don't always trust his support, though, because even if his words communicate steady endorsement of what you have to do to succeed in your career, he has an uncanny ability to say things that make you feel bad about working.

How does the "guilter" husband really feel about your absence from home? Does he wish that you'd come to your senses and come home like a good wife? Why doesn't he just tell you what he wants, instead of taking subtle stabs at your conscience? Will you ever be able to pursue your career without feeling pulled back home? Maybe if he weren't such a good guy, it would be easier to feel righteous and indignant about working so many hours away from home, but it's precisely because your husband is mostly a peach that your ambivalence is amplified.

One quick tip: Recognize that a husband who is a master at "guilting" you has power over you only when you give it to him. The problem is not his alone (although he owns a share of it) but yours as well. He couldn't make you feel so guilty if you were at peace with the personal and family sacrifices you're making in order to be successful in your career. You may wish you could be cuddled up with your sweetheart or tucking your children into bed when work demands that you be elsewhere. The person who must change in this scenario is you. You must learn to find enough meaning and prosperity in your work to make your absence regrettable but a price worth paying, or make changes at work to bring you home more often.

The next time your husband says something that pushes one of your hot buttons, feel grateful rather than irritated. It's glorious that your husband and children still need you and that you still miss them, and that, as a working wife, you have the privilege of a full life. Feel compassion for single women with no one tugging at them to come home, and be thankful you haven't become a coldhearted businesswoman who doesn't miss her family. Remember the working wives whose husbands don't care whether they come home or not. Then bless your husband, even when it's difficult, and don't give him the power to make you feel guilty about the hard choices you've made in your life.

4. The Withdrawer/Withholder ("Leave me alone right now—I don't want to talk about it.")

This husband isn't fighting you with nasty words. He's pulled away from you, emotionally and physically. You may be getting the silent treatment. He may start spending more time at work or with friends. You may be concerned he is having an affair or is thinking about it. Or he may withdraw into an addictive pastime such as gambling, television watching, or drinking.

This husband withholds money, affection, sex, verbal approval, and compliments as a form of punishment. His message is, "If you are going to abandon me or treat me poorly, then I'm not going to give you what you need." He is essentially having a silent temper tantrum. He manipulates you by giving you what you crave only when you give him what he

> Over the many years I've been doing this show, the number one complaint I hear is that "he doesn't communicate."
>
> —Oprah Winfrey,
> television personality

wants. He's essentially asking you to reduce your commitment to work so he can feel reassured and loved again, but he hasn't said so with his words, just his actions.

We aren't accustomed to thinking of being ignored as a form of abuse, but ask the clients who are paying their therapists hundreds of dollars to heal from the effects of emotional abandonment by their parents or spouses if they would agree. We long more than anything to be "seen" and validated by the people to whom we are closest. Feeling invisible or not listened to can be just as painful as direct abuse.

Although we could describe this kind of marital relationship as a failure to communicate, a husband or wife who silently stews and refuses to engage in lovemaking or conversation is communicating plenty. Silence in a marriage may be a well-intentioned attempt to keep the marriage together. When one or both members of the couple are angry and distant, they may worry honesty could shatter the relationship. They may be feeling, "Better to pull away than speak, because my spouse isn't really ready to hear what's on my mind." Silence that is intended to punish a partner or avoid a critical issue, however, will almost never produce a positive result.

One quick tip: John Gray, Ph.D., author of the groundbreaking book *Men Are from Mars, Women Are from Venus,* believes that men sometimes retreat to a "cave" to think and solve problems. According to Dr. Gray, women need to give men time and space to get ready to talk, rather than prodding, pursuing, or scolding them. Couples quickly get entrenched in pursuer/withdrawer roles, a dynamic that becomes more intense the longer it continues. If you pursue your husband when he withdraws, he will probably run away even faster. If you continue to chase him, he may spend most of his time and energy trying to get away from you. Men "come out" when they are ready—when they feel loved, respected, and accepted. Wise up. Dragging a man out of his cave never works, even when it appears to be the only solution. You might take a hostage, but you'll never have a willing, equal partner that way.

5. The Competitor/Criticizer ("I've been in business a lot longer than you, and what you're doing is stupid. It'll never work.")

If you asked me to choose which of the five resistant male behaviors is the most destructive to a woman's psyche, I'd have to say it's this one. The critical, competitive guy is most apt to destroy her self-esteem, knocking the confidence out of her. The passive-aggressive husband annoys her, the incompetent exhausts her, the guilter pulls on her heartstrings, and the withdrawer leaves her frustrated and lonely. But the competitor/criticizer is like a termite eating at the structure of the marriage. If his nibbling is allowed to continue for too long, the whole house will come crashing down.

This guy's ego must be managed. He is used to being center stage, and he has to be right, no matter what. His wife is an opponent, not an ally. He lives in a hierarchical universe of one up or one down; if his wife is successful in her work, he has to be more successful or he's a loser.

> Research has shown that men usually sleep on the right side of the bed. Even in their sleep they have to be right.
>
> —Rita Rudner, comedian

If you are married to such a man, he may work longer hours at work to show you that his career is more demanding or important than yours. He may launch a new business or go after a promotion at the precise moment that you feel overwhelmed with work demands and caring for the children. Your marriage feels like competition on every level. The content of your arguments scarcely matters—it's all about winning and taking control.

Scott Haltzman, M.D., an expert on male psychology, shares his insight into the way some men find their place in the world:

> Being a man is a process that must be earned, and then proven. Think about how societies celebrate manhood; it is tied to achievement. While primitive cultures might ask the boy-man to complete a hunting feat or act of strength, even in American culture, manhood is tested by physical acts. A boy can attain adult status by getting drunk, getting laid, or even engaging in a drive-by shooting. This status must be proven again and again. It doesn't suffice to tell my frat friends that I established my manhood last semester by getting drunk, so I don't have to do it anymore. The challenge of placing yourself in the public eye and judgment of others, and coming out on top, is an ongoing one. "Are you man enough?" is not a question answered only once.

In contrast to the passive-aggressive husband, who is generous with apologies, this husband would rather get a root canal than apologize, because saying "I'm sorry" is admitting fault and places his wife in a superior position. If you demand an apology from him—even if you deserve one and he knows it—he'll stand his ground and fire back, finding the words to make you wrong. This is a man who blames others and is unable to take responsibility for his contribution to problems.

The competitor/criticizer may belittle your accomplishments, ridicule you with name-calling, and point out your weaknesses at every opportunity. He will joke about you to others ("Just kidding, honey"), tell you that you are not entitled to feel what you feel (invalidation), or blanket you with one complaint after another (the soup isn't salty enough, your butt is getting fat, the kitchen floor doesn't shine). It's an endless stream of nastiness.

This sort of husband may be threatened by the independence that your work gives you. If you are financially less dependent on him and are meeting other men at work, he risks losing you. Ironically, it's not your work that threatens the marriage but his poor treatment of you, but he doesn't see it that way unless he gets a wake-up call.

> When your husband says something hurtful to you, respond by saying "ouch" and then leave the room if you can. When you don't punish him for his comment by hurting him back, you preserve your dignity and the potential for intimacy and peace.
>
> —Laura Doyle,
> *Surrendered Wife*

A part of you knows that the abuse is his problem, not yours, but a constant barrage of criticism from your so-called beloved can't help but crack your armor. Over time, you may begin to agree with him or find that your self-esteem has been destroyed. It is impossible to put your best foot forward at work when your husband is constantly tripping you up at home. Unless you are a robot, he's going to get to you. The questions are, how can you protect yourself, and what can you do to get him to stop? What does he need that you can give him without compromising your integrity?

O UR SAGES call upon the wife to honor her husband. I know that honoring may smack of servility and sound outdated, but mutual respect is the foundation upon which marriage should be built. If respect is lacking in a relationship, love will quickly dissipate, but when honor and respect prevail, love will grow and flourish.

—Rebettzin Jungreis, *The Committed Life*

One quick tip: As difficult as it can be to accomplish, if you intend to stay married to a man who constantly criticizes and belittles you, you must distance yourself from his criticism as if you were witnessing it in a movie. Concentrate on this irony: Your husband's criticisms of you are likely rooted in your strengths, not your weaknesses. Your strengths illuminate his flaws, which shames him enough that he has to make this problem about you and your deficits, rather than acknowledge his own. So, consider this twisted logic: The more he comes down on you for not being good enough, the more excellent you must be!

As I've said before, if the verbal abuse gets out of hand or he hurts you physically, seek professional help and leave the marriage. But if you're married to a basically decent guy who still loves you, and you still love him and feel that your marriage is worth saving, the strategies we discuss in this book can work with even the harshest, most critical husbands. Your husband cannot celebrate your excellence and give you the approval you crave until he, too, feels like a winner.

Your husband may have positive intentions, even if it doesn't seem like it to you. It's tempting to see your own good intentions but assume that your partner is self-centered or cruel, wanting only to hurt you or get in your way.

Your spouse may indeed be self-centered. But you may also be missing his attempts to care for you, because those attempts don't look like you think they should. Is it reasonable to assume that your intentions are always positive but his are negative? Like you, he shifts in and out of watching out for himself and trying to protect you.

The critical guy who troubles you now is also the man to whom you once declared your undying love. Same guy! So, if you don't want to throw him away and hope for better luck next time around, what can you do to improve your relationship with your husband?

Remember the serenity prayer: "God, grant me the serenity to accept the things I cannot change, the courage to change the things I can, and the wisdom to know the difference."

For the rest of this book, you'll learn how to accept those aspects of your husband you wish you could change—but can't. You'll learn new strategies to give you the courage to change the negative behaviors in your marriage. There is plenty you can do with, and without, your husband's cooperation to improve your marriage.

I hope you'll develop the wisdom to know when it's time to work on changing your marriage and when it's time to relax and accept with gratitude the blessings you have. What you focus on is indeed what you will see. If you are married to a man who wants to love you but needs help knowing how, before he can become your ideal man, he needs reassurance from you that you are committed to him for life and that he is loved and accepted for who he is. I know this reassurance is difficult to offer when you are feeling unloved by your husband. Try an experiment—treat him as if he were the husband you've always wanted. Then maybe he might surprise you with who he can become—and who you will become as a result will inspire him even more! The first step to creating a positive spiral in your marriage begins with you.

CHAPTER FOUR

The Trouble Doesn't Always Start with Him

How Your Behavior
May Be Contributing to the Problem

ISN'T IT tempting to make the permission-to-prosper issue about self-centered, stubborn men who won't support their wives? But after hours of research (and having used a microscope on my own behavior), I am compelled to draw a different conclusion: Wives create a lot of the trouble. This is actually good news; it means we can fix it.

There is no question that many women do not have their husbands' full support—permission to prosper in their chosen careers—and yearn to find ways to receive it while still enjoying an intimate and satisfying emotional connection with the men they love. It is also true that, as we learned in the chapter 3, some husbands respond to their working wives in ways that are downright hurtful. Still, if all your energy is focused on finding ways to change your husband, you are likely to be deeply disappointed.

You can succeed in your career, and perhaps even find happiness, without your husband's approval or enthusiastic support. You can learn to detach yourself so his feelings don't control your life. But do you really want to? Most women want both—permission to prosper in their life's work and an intimate, mutually satisfying connection with a supportive and loving husband—without sacrificing one for the other. How can you achieve a prosperous and fulfilling career and build a marriage in which you and your husband are each other's biggest fan? Are you willing to change your own behavior to accomplish that goal?

This chapter will help you understand some of the well-intentioned but ineffective ways you may be pushing your partner's buttons. It will also show you strategies to increase your odds of getting the permission to prosper that you crave.

When we worship the god of "being right and in charge" at the expense of marital intimacy, we discover quickly that a controlled husband is never an amorous one. Many a wife fears that if she doesn't control her husband, her needs will be unmet, but her controlling behavior *ensures* that he does not meet her needs. Together in this chapter, we will learn how to trade the potential rewards of being "in control" for the greater reward of deeper intimacy with our husbands.

Let's look at five ineffective behaviors working wives often use to get what they desire from their husbands. You will be able to learn from them all, even if one or two might resonate for you more than others.

1. The Egalitarian ("This isn't fair!")

You're too tired for sex three times a week. How does he expect you to cook him dinner like you used to after working forty hours a week and fighting rush-hour traffic to get home?

You used to cuddle up and watch your favorite television show together, but now, after getting the kids into bed (with no help from him), you fall asleep by the first commercial.

Many working wives put in a full day and then arrive home to another three or four hours a night of domestic duties. Many believe their husbands should pitch in and help—and many are filled with resentment that their husbands do not seem to believe the same thing. You were there for him when his business zapped a lot of his energy. Why can't he be more helpful now, when you need a break from putting his mental and physical well-being first? It's only fair! This is supposed to be a partnership, but he's not fulfilling his end of the bargain.

> When you use fairness and equality as a measure within your marriage, you don't have a marriage, you have a contest.
>
> —Susan Page,
> *If We're So in Love,*
> *Why Aren't We Happy?*

You need a "wife" to meet your needs so that your career can prosper, but hubby isn't stepping up to the plate. You were sure when you married your husband that he was "one of the good ones" and that your marriage would be a true and equal partnership.

Your disappointment, even devastation, at the loss of your dream of an "equal partnership" may color every interaction you have with your husband. Your daily exhaustion makes the relationship seem even worse than it is. You may be obsessed with what you are entitled to, rather than what you can give.

I am not saying you are wrong. You do deserve his help, and it probably isn't "fair." But insisting that you're entitled and complaining about all the ways your husband lets you down are unlikely to inspire greater effort on his part.

Rabbi Shraga Simmons of Cleveland summarizes this problem succinctly:

> Years ago, when I was getting married, I went to one of the biggest sages in Jerusalem and asked, "What's the key to a successful, happy marriage?"
>
> He told me that the secret is to be a giver. Because if you come into marriage asking, "What will she do for me?" then you're pulling in the opposite direction, away from your spouse. But if you come in asking, "What can I do to provide and contribute?" then that builds a connection. And if both partners approach marriage with this same attitude, then the relationship flows beautifully in both directions.
>
> Today we live in a society where everyone seems concerned about his rights: "What's in it for me? What do I get out of it?"

When you are feeling unsupported, exhausted, and overwhelmed, it is difficult to consider what you can do for your husband. You want him to be thinking about what he can do for you. You'll never achieve that goal by banging him over the head with the fact that he owes it to you.

When discussing the concept of equal partnership, most women focus their attention on child care and housework. For instance, he should wash the dishes in the sink if you've cooked the meal, or he should give the kids a bath before you read them their bedtime stories. But equality is much more than that. Your chances are slim of getting a husband who splits the child care and housework responsibilities fifty-fifty, unless he is a stay-at-home dad.

You probably want your husband to respect you as an intelligent adult and to consult you about work, his family, health, religious commitments, parenting, and your relationship. You want him to involve you in his day-to-day life and to think about how he can make your life easier. You want him to be willing to make sacrifices to enable you to prosper in your career, because your career counts as much as his. You want to be able to depend on him for those areas of expertise that are beyond you, such as auto maintenance, lawn care, or making that outrageous chocolate mousse of his.

You want to know that you can rely on your beloved to stick by you should you ever suffer a disabling illness or accident. You want a voice in any financial or career decisions he makes that affect your life. You want both of you to be equally respected members of the same team.

If you are married to a decent guy, you can create the feeling of equal partnership in your marriage even if he never washes the dishes—but only if you expand your thinking about what an equal partnership looks and feels like. One of the worst mistakes working wives make is that they harp on the few aspects of unequal partnership their husbands are least apt to change, instead of nurturing the ways they can achieve the feeling of partnership that they crave.

If you want your husband to treat you as an equal partner, consider your own behavior. If you're nagging or complaining, stop. Be sure to express appreciation for what he does do. Ask him for his help with respect and courtesy. And be willing to offer the same respect, courtesy, and support that you expect from him. The Golden Rule is still valid; treat your husband as you would like to be treated, and see what happens.

2. The Martyr ("I'll do it myself if I want it done right!")

Your husband offers to help, but he doesn't do things to your standards. You don't trust him to watch the children; he dresses them oddly and lets them watch too much television. You want domestic tasks done in a particular way, so you do them all yourself—but then you feel exhausted and resentful. Your frustration with your husband may be misplaced. The problem isn't entirely his unwillingness to help but also your inability or refusal to give up control and to delegate tasks on what was once your turf.

You may turn a willing husband into a dependent or resistant one if you insist on supervising and criticizing each aspect of every task around the house. Failing to notice what he does do or exaggerating the problem ("You never play with the children when you're watching them" or "I always have to make dinner") doesn't help either.

> Don't feel totally, personally, irrevocably, eternally responsible for everything. That's my job.
>
> —God

Before you "educate your husband" about how to be more helpful, take a look at your motive. Are you trying to teach him a skill, bolstering the equal partnership you say you want, or are you unconsciously giving him every reason to hand the task back to you so that you can return to your familiar role as the martyr wife of a lazy, unsupportive husband? If you want his permission to prosper, you have to allow him to give it to you.

If it seems like you are doing what is necessary only because your husband fights you every step of the way, your steamy arguments may stem at times from your choice of language. You may attack your husband with statements like "You *never* say anything nice to me or compliment me on the way I look" or "You get your way *every* time we argue!"

In response to your exaggerated statements, he feels righteous about responding with his logical evidence that you are wrong, because he can easily point out an exception to your always/never language. Don't give him this opportunity—catch yourself *every* time you hear the word "always" or "never" rolling off your tongue. (And yes, I mean *every* time!)

If your husband is like a turtle tentatively poking his head out of his shell and trying out "women's work" because he wants to be helpful, when you attack him for doing it all wrong, he'll retreat quickly into his shell and give you what you may be unconsciously seeking—full control once again, because he's not going to do it anymore. You have won—or have you?

The "poor me" role is a very difficult one to give up when you are fueled by the adrenaline rush of getting twenty things done in one evening and comforted by the sense of control that comes from managing the household to your liking. What's dangerous, and ultimately unfair to your husband, is that you can give away too much of yourself and then, because of your built-up resentment, emotionally leave your marriage.

We'll address how to share household and parenting responsibilities in later chapters. The first step, which can actually make you more hopeful about your marriage, is to realize that your husband might be more willing and capable than you've given him credit for—if you'll let go of the power that being a martyr gives you.

3. The Independent ("I can take care of myself now!")

Declaring independence worked well for the thirteen American colonies, but sometimes it's harmful to a marriage. As we have learned, marriage is about moving from two *I*'s to one *we*. If you focus on your own independence, your spouse may focus on his independence as well. Before you know it, you are merely roommates with separate lives, not lovers or friends.

George Pransky, author of *Divorce Is Not the Answer,* teaches:

> The feeling state that you present to people hooks either their ego or their altruism. If you are in a state of angry indignation, others will fight you tooth and nail. If you are in a state of deep gratitude, others will pull out all the stops to help. As your level of goodwill rises, people become ever more cooperative.

Let's say that you are so determined to prove that you can manage your career yourself that you don't ask for his opinion and you act as if he is entirely unnecessary. Perhaps he starts thinking, "Now that she's earning a good living, the only thing she needs me from me is to mow the lawn. And she can hire someone to do that." He doesn't see how your career success will benefit him; in fact, it seems to be taking you further away from him. Your work, which is fueling your growing independence, becomes the enemy. Your husband might wholeheartedly support your journey to prosperity, but only if he won't lose you as a result.

Vicki expresses the attitude of a wife who is more interested in the health of her marriage than her own independence:

One of the reasons that I wanted to start my own business was so my husband wouldn't have to drive the long miles he drives every day to work. I'm hoping that he can quit his job once my business gets profitable, because there are so few jobs in our area. Even though this is my business, my husband surprised me by asking to be named a partner in the business. That meant a lot to me. It means that we're in this together.

Vicki had plenty of personal motivation to become an entrepreneur. Eighty percent of her motivation was selfish in nature—she hated her previous job. But she gave her husband his 20 percent. She included him in her planning, asked for his advice, and helped him see how he also would benefit from her work. From the beginning of her business, it was a *we* venture, even though it was really *her* business.

You may argue that your husband has no expertise whatsoever in your line of work, and asking for his advice would be counterproductive, since he doesn't understand the business and might advise you poorly. You could still choose to educate him so that he can be helpful, find some aspect of the business where he can offer some useful advice, or ask him to be a sounding board without offering any advice at all. He may not understand finance, but he can listen to your concerns about an unproductive employee. Don't wait until your business plans are fully developed before conversing with him about them.

Robin Ryan, one of the nation's top career experts and author of several bestselling books, is married to a busy chiropractor. Although she and her husband operate in entirely different universes during the day, they value each other as intelligent professionals and consult with each other often for work-related concerns. Robin shared this:

Stephen and I set up telephone meetings during his lunch hour at work, since our young son makes it difficult to discuss work at home. We'll discuss marketing or employee issues, or run new ideas and problems by each other. This helps us feel like partners who are involved in each other's work, which is a mainstay in our lives besides our son.

Vicki tried the independent route, but it wasn't working for her, so her husband stepped in for a welcome rescue, as she explained:

I have a weak spot when it comes to numbers, whereas my husband is a civil engineer; working with numbers is second nature to him. I was trying to put together a sales forecast for my business plan, tearing my hair out over it for days and snapping at him. Eventually he asked what was driving me mental. When I sat down and showed him, he started to draw it out on a graph for me, which made it easier to understand and compile. I've now asked him to be in charge of the accounting side of things, as I just don't have the knack for it.

Some of you will offer this valid objection: "My husband doesn't want me to work or to own my own business. I am not sharing anything with him, because he'll only shoot me down."

You may be perpetuating a vicious cycle by shutting your husband out of your life and declaring your independence from his involvement. In fact, you may incur his wrath about your work because he sees it as the cause of your distance from him. This is a time for self-reflection. Are you viewing your work as a means to get financial or emotional independence from your husband? Are you ambivalent about your marriage? If so, you shouldn't expect your husband's full support along the way.

If financial independence is your motivation and you don't want to deal with your husband's resistance every time you turn around, look for ways to let your husband know you respect and need him even while you strive to build your career.

Your husband's criticism may lead you to approach your work with an "I'll show you!" attitude. You may feel compelled to reject your husband's help (even when you need it) because you fear being told, "I told you so." When you discover that career or business demands are more than you expected, lean on your life partner to give you some emotional sustenance, even if he warned you that this idea might not work. Being independent is not all it's cracked up to be, or we'd all be single.

> When evaluating a potential job change, 42 percent of executives would first seek the advice of their spouse or significant other before going to a mentor, coworker, or friend.
>
> —From a 2002 Accountemps survey of 150 executives at the nation's 1,000 largest companies

4. The Dedicated Mama ("The kids need me more than you do.")

Your so-called leisure hours outside of work are scarce, and you are raising children. You miss your kids terribly and feel guilty about the hours you are absent from their lives. You tell yourself that your husband can manage fine without you, but kids need a mother's guidance. Any free time you have outside of work goes to them. You become a career woman and a mother, and you stop being a wife—except for the rare evenings when you "agree" to have sex so your husband won't climb the walls.

A young child does need you more than your husband does, but in different ways. Your husband is an independent adult who can feed himself, do his own laundry, and make a life for himself far more easily than your children can. Balancing your commitment to your children, your husband, and your career is not easy, but it's risky to focus on one or two at the expense of the others. You may not be able to predict when your husband's heart will be open to you—and when he might decide that your decision to focus on your work and the children at his expense entitles him to spend his energies elsewhere as well. Romance, sexual connection, and friendship are not naturally present in a marriage just because you live together. They wither and die from disuse. (We will learn more about balancing parenting and work in chapter 6.)

Beware of the common mistake working wives make of prioritizing their careers and their children over their husbands. You may discover that the children grow up, the jobs come and go, and you are alone later in life, when you would most appreciate companionship. A marriage is like a garden that needs constant watering. If you plant no flowers and let the weeds grow for years, then show up with a whole truckload full of fertilizer once your career demands less of you and the children have grown, all you'll get are bigger weeds. Once the weeds have taken over the garden, it's difficult to remove them so flowers can grow again. It's much easier to tend the garden, even for just a few moments a week, so that the weeds don't ever have a chance to take over.

In chapter 7 you will learn ways to improve your sexual and romantic connection. Even if the children need most of your waking hours outside of work, you can still find ways to make your husband feel that he is your number one priority.

5. The Criticizer ("If only you would change!")

You may be stressed-out by your career and convinced that most of the problems in your life could be eliminated if your husband would get his act together. You continually tell him he is letting you down, making your life more difficult, embarrassing or annoying you, and otherwise being a drag. You bought this book because you believe that if you could just fix your husband, everything in your life would work better. Nothing you do seems to change him; you feel dissatisfied and powerless.

What you have no doubt discovered is that your complaints and criticism don't do a darn thing to make your husband more supportive. If anything, he seems to be getting worse. You hate the bitch you have become, and so does he. Michele Weiner-Davis, author of *Divorce Busting,* says it well: "I've never met a man who, after being accused of having the same undesirable trait as his parent, reflects upon his behavior and genuinely says, 'Thank you for your insightful comments, dear. I'll work on that.'"

You know that the incessant arguing has to stop. When you think about living together like this for the rest of your life, you feel despair. You want your best friend back. But how can you get him to change without constantly pointing out his shortcomings?

Here's a news flash: Criticism will never shape your husband into the lover and friend you desire. Criticism does not work, will never work, and has never worked. It may be impossible to give up criticism entirely, but you can reduce the intensity and frequency of your criticism and develop an internal witness who will listen to your occasional tirades, tap you on the shoulder, and whisper in your ear, "Pssst, this isn't going to work. It'll only make things worse. Remember?"

Arlie Russell Hochschild, author of *The Second Shift*, reminds us, "The scariest part about surrendering to your husband is that it may seem like you're never going to get your way, but just the opposite is true. When you give up unnecessary control of things your husband does—how he drives, what he wears, what he does at work, how he loads the dishwasher—you actually gain power in the relationship and in your life. When he feels respected, his natural instinct to provide, protect, and adore you comes back."

> Every woman is entitled to her bottom line: the absolute essentials she will not compromise for the sake of being in an intimate relationship. The trouble is that some women have so much on their bottom line.
>
> —A. Justin Sterling,
> *What Really Works with Men*

You may have wonderful intentions when you criticize your mate. When you want to feel closer to your husband, more cherished and loved, more supported, and happier in your marriage, the last thing that will bring you that result is criticism—even though you are convinced that if he fixed some negative traits, he would be a happier human being and a better husband. It's your job as his wife to influence him in a positive direction. Behind every great man is a woman, right?

Not necessarily. Focus on solutions, rather than harp on problems. Be specific in your requests. You know what you mean when you ask your husband to help with the kids' bedtime routine—but does he? What does he hear when you say, "I need you to help me with the kids' bedtime routine before you fall asleep"?

He may hear, "You are a lazy slob who does nothing around here to help me. I'm tired from working all day, and you should be helping me more around the house. I expect you to stay awake until all of the kids' homework is done and their showers are finished." Instead of whining, be specific. Ask your husband to help your oldest son review his math homework, for example, or make sure that the kids have taken a shower. A smile and a pleasant tone of voice will help. Maybe you're willing to handle the rest, and he can fall asleep after those two items are covered, but he won't know that unless you tell him.

Your husband's resistance to giving you what you want is rooted in many things. He may believe that he can never please you, no matter what he does. Or he may be convinced that your requests are unreasonable. He has also learned to tune you out because you are harping on the same issues and a nasty tone of voice makes him feel defensive, rather than cooperative. He doesn't hear a request; he hears a complaint, which does not ignite in him any desire to make you happy. (It may, however, ignite in him a desire to get away from you.)

Your husband's annoying traits may just be a different orientation to relating in the world. We would hate it if our husbands spent as much energy trying to change us as we focus on them.

The way to get what you want is to treat your husband with so much respect, kindness, dignity, and acceptance that his cup is overflowing with love, prompting him to want to please you, rather than having to be roped into it. When he does something for you because he cares for you and wants to make you happy, it's a solid commitment without negative repercussions; it's not a threat to his ego, because he is making a personal choice out of love.

The only way to get your husband to change is to love and accept him for who he is, foibles and all. Andrew Christensen, Ph.D., coauthor of *Reconcilable Differences,* writes, "Change is the brother of acceptance, but it is the younger brother. When acceptance comes first, it paves the way for change."

I read a joke once that made me laugh at its message: "What three things does a bride think of as she walks down the aisle in church on her wedding day? Aisle, altar, hymn (I'll alter him)." I'd like to say that I've been exempt from this tendency, since as a Jew I wasn't married in a church, but alas, its truth applies equally well to me.

Trust me. You can create your dream relationship with this imperfect man of yours by accepting him as he is, stopping the criticism, and letting go of unreasonable expectations. You can gently coach and inspire him to become the husband you desire.

Healthy Ground Rules
for Handling Conflict in Any Marriage

IF YOU are dissatisfied with the current state of your marriage (and who among us doesn't feel that way sometimes?), consider the following suggestions:

1. When you are troubled, you may be tempted to groan to your girlfriends. Only a wise friend will have the courage to point out to you the ways you may be contributing to the problem.

When your marriage is rocky, seek out friends who will remind you of what is worth saving about your marriage. You may need to find a skilled therapist or clergy who can help you find real solutions, ways to heal your marriage and draw you and your husband closer together.

2. If you think that the solution to your marital problems is better communication, be careful. More communication, if it is not loving and skillful, will backfire. When you learn how to converse as respectful, considerate, loving adults, rather than agitated, spiteful adversaries, you can make serious progress. But never confuse complaining and "getting it out in the open" with better communication. Real communication also involves listening and the willingness of both partners to change and grow.

> Problems are like goldfish. The more you feed them, the bigger they get.
>
> —George Pransky, *Divorce Is Not the Answer*

3. Be grateful for temporary improvements, even if you don't get everything you want. If your husband does change and you either don't notice or fail to offer your appreciation, he may think, "Why should I bother when she doesn't even seem to notice?" Don't let a long history of problems or stored-up resentment keep you from noticing and encouraging even small changes in the right direction.

Try to see the negative behaviors as the anomaly, rather than to view the new positive behaviors as the exception. In marriage, as in so many other things, attitude truly is everything.

Have you ever noticed that hours of analyzing and dissecting your relationship can be counterproductive? Sometimes it is better to take the focus off the problems you are never going to solve (no matter how much you analyze them) and spotlight instead any remaining beauty, joy, and satisfaction in your relationship.

Whatever you shine your mental flashlight on will be what occupies your mind. An amazing thing happens when you stop focusing on all of your problems and complaints. Without any conscious effort, your relationship can get a lot better!

Become "Unbummable"

YOU'VE FIGURED out by now that I'm not going to encourage you to strive for independence from your husband. I want you to know that your craving for his approval and friendship is natural, thousands of years in the making. He is your mate for life—we hope—and you cannot be truly happy in your life if your happiness comes at the expense of his. You want to share a vision with him, instead of charting your own course and hoping that he won't get in your way. You need your husband to be the wind in your sails, not the hole in your boat that sinks you.

You don't need to give up what you truly need in order to keep your man happy. You only have to figure out what's in it for him, too, and help him see that by supporting you in your goals, he will have a happier wife and a more fulfilling marriage. If you put your career aspirations on ice to please your man, he won't have a truly happy wife, which is really what he wants. Sometimes, also, you can be too sensitive to your husband's state of mind. If your mood lifts and drops along with your husband's mood and you have no firm sense of self apart from him, you will be forever controlled by your husband's whims and, most of the time, miserable. You can learn to feel serenity and joy as you build your career, even when your husband is angry or depressed, without isolating yourself from him. You can stay connected, even intimate, and still maintain a healthy sense of self.

For example, I can measure with my husband's laughter how I am doing with this. When my husband is grumpy, his lighthearted laughter disappears and a cloud comes over the house. When he's in a funk, I struggle mightily to lift my mood in his presence, especially when he lashes out at me in frustration. When his laughter returns to the house, I feel palpable relief: "Stephen's back. Thank God."

I am sometimes too sensitive to my husband's moods, but I'd rather err in that direction and still keep trying to bring back his laughter than to be overly self-centered in our relationship. My goal is to reach a point in our relationship where I become unbummable by my husband's mood swings, which is far different from striving for independence from him as my life partner.

Dissatisfaction and grumpiness are like the flu—sometimes spouses catch them from each other. When you believe that your home and your marriage are a haven and your husband is your biggest cheerleader, he can sneeze a grumpy mood at you, and you can respond by making him some chicken soup and giving him a hug, instead of catching the grumpy flu yourself.

Being unbummable means learning to protect yourself from catching your husband's every mood. You can get professional help if you need it; you can develop a network of supportive friends and family, engage in meaningful work and enjoyable play, and cultivate a loving, stable marriage that nurtures your soul and gives you a reason to wake up each morning.

You can learn the artful dance between caring for your husband's feelings and concerns and nurturing your own joy and satisfaction in life. Even if he is struggling and not giving you the approval or permission to prosper you desire, you can choose to act in ways that invite his love and support.

CHAPTER FIVE

Money and Stress

W HAT KIND of marriage did your parents have? Was your father the provider and your mother a stay-at-home mom? Did your mother work only after the youngest children were enrolled in school, or did she work "mothers' hours" so that she could greet you with milk and cookies when you hopped off the school bus? Did your parents work together in the same business as equal partners, or was your father always considered "the boss"?

With the exception of low-income homes where adults work several jobs just to provide food and shelter, the cultural norm for eons in this country has been that the husband's paycheck provides the family's bread and butter; any income earned by the wife is secondary and, ideally, optional.

We now have a new normal. According to recent government statistics, an estimated 10.5 million women, or about 30 percent of working wives, outearn their spouses—twice the rate of twenty years ago—and this number is expected to rise. A 2002 report from the Center for Women's Business

Research and Wells Fargo reports that the number of women-owned businesses continues to rise at double the rate of all U.S. businesses, growing 14 percent between 1997 and 2002 and totaling 6.2 million businesses nationwide. A 2002 report from the Center for Women's Business Research indicates that 1.2 million businesses in the United States are owned by women of color, up 31.5 percent since 1997.

Twenty years ago, a woman was most likely to achieve security by making a "good catch" in a husband. Today women are more likely to echo this professional woman, who makes a statement frequently heard these days from women in their twenties and thirties: "I purposely chose the computer field because my mom, a mother of eight children, always told me, 'Never depend on a man to support you.' So I chose a field that I knew would yield a solid career, regardless of whether I found someone to love or not." The new brand of woman marries for love, not money, because she can earn her own money now.

> If a woman marries a man who earns more than her, everyone congratulates her for making a good choice. If he earns less than her, everyone asks him how he copes with it.
>
> —Olivia Mellan,
> *Money Shy to Money Sure*

Women are now selecting and succeeding in careers that are lucrative enough to free them from the yoke of dependence on a man. It offends many women even to suggest that they need a man for anything except making a baby. That's about the only job left that can't be taken away from him—and at the rate that medical science is evolving, who knows what's in store for our children's generation.

Just twenty years ago, the response to this book would have been, "Women aren't concerned with prospering. Their families and husbands come first. Prospering is the husband's concern." Not any longer. Prospering is now a woman's issue, too.

A woman's career may be just as important to her as her husband's, or even more so. She may shoulder more of the responsibility for paying bills. And she may find herself married to a guy who takes it personally that his wife "has" to work. No one denies the significant impact that women's entrée into the workforce has had on today's marriages.

Every day now, the media feature entrepreneurial wives and their husbands and ask them how they manage the stress on their marriages. Or they profile the unusual stay-at-home dad who sits among a group of mothers at the playground or runs a home-based business while he watches the kids after school. Expressions like "the glass ceiling" and "breadwinner wife" are part of our daily vocabulary; daytime talk shows continually address the phenomenon of the changing role of women.

The primary reason all of this is such a big deal is money. Money—who earns it, who spends it, and who controls it— is power. It isn't his wife's income that threatens a husband's ego but rather what it says about his earning power and his ability to count on his wife's sticking around.

Money not only pays the electric bill and puts groceries on the table; it also enables a woman to build a prosperous life for herself without a husband (or perhaps in spite of her husband). Marrying a man is no longer her ticket to luxury or security—in fact, he might prevent her from achieving wealth on her own. Without a husband nagging her to come home at night, she could work longer hours without guilt and prosper at twice the rate.

Women's rights in the workplace now extend to the home as well. The woman who fifty years ago didn't question washing the kitchen floor each day is now more likely to hire someone to do it, to live without a clean floor, or to pressure her husband to clean the floor half of the time.

Women have so thoroughly adopted the notion of unlimited opportunities and equal rights that the notion of their needing a husband's permission to prosper doesn't sit well with them. It feels too much like being subservient to a husband. Some women become so insistent on financial power that they run a substantial risk of being alone—never married, divorced, married with no children, or in a marriage devoid of intimacy. *True power is being able to choose the life that you want.* Working wives often remain confused about how to create an abundant life that includes a meaningful career, a loving husband, and happy, thriving children. If they desire parenthood, successful female executives with all the money they need, but no family connections, often feel anything but abundant.

A 2002 study, by the University of Michigan Institute for Social Research, of 611 midlife moms revealed that two-thirds of those surveyed felt that they had been less successful in their work lives than their adult daughters. They also felt that their daughters were less happy than they themselves had been at the same age. Money in the bank and more opportunities at work do not automatically create a happy woman, any more than they guarantee a happy man. (Ask any workaholic man with an unsatisfying marriage how happy he is.)

Consider the couple who appeared on a recent television program. The wife, an attorney, had been fighting with her husband, a UPS deliveryman, for all seven years of their marriage. She said, "I've been divorcing him since the year after we got married, but I haven't left him yet. Initially it was a scare tactic, the most volatile thing I could say to win the argument, but now I'm starting to mean it."

Why has she been divorcing him since the honeymoon was over? Her lawyer's salary gave her the power to walk out anytime she wanted to, and her husband knew that. She didn't need him—or so it seemed.

Her core complaint was that her husband criticized her every waking moment at home, from how she loaded the dishwasher to how she mothered their children. She said, "I graduated summa cum laude from law school, but at home I feel like a complete fool; I can't do anything right."

When this woman finally spoke directly to her husband, she said, "The feminist in me is laughing, but I need you to approve of me, to like me, to feel proud of me. I need you clapping for me. You are my best friend, and when you aren't cheering for me, my peanut gallery is empty. The only person whose opinion has ever mattered to me is yours. When you attack me, I feel worthless and discarded. I feel like the life force in me is empty. If I knew that you were proud of me and of who I am and what I do every day, it would make me feel alive again. I feel like I'm dying."

Her bank account was full, but her life force was depleted. She felt like she was dying because her husband had not dealt with his insecurities. Inept at handling his unconscious fears, he aimed to make her feel small so that he would feel bigger. And he had succeeded. But had he really gotten what he wanted? Had either of them?

Who really had power in this relationship? She had money and independence—she could pay the bills without

> IN THE early years of our marriage, I viewed my earnings as mine, and Stephen's (my husband) as ours. I wanted to be equal partners, but I also wanted him to take care of me. I wanted him to respect my work, but I didn't want us to depend on my income. It took a long time, and quite a few arguments, to realize I couldn't have it both ways.
>
> —Peggy Orenstein, *Flux*

her husband—but he retained the power in the relationship, the ability to make her "feel like a fool" for not loading the dishwasher properly.

An increase in women's wages has not necessarily made women more powerful. The feminists in us are screaming in frustration, because all of our money hasn't wiped out our yearning to be approved of by our husbands. Years ago we could have gotten that need met by keeping the house clean, looking beautiful, and raising the children well. Now our husbands' approval is more elusive.

Money tension is inevitable in a dual-career marriage, where husbands and wives are still sorting out what it really means to them that the wife is working outside of the home. Following are a few of the common themes. Which most applies to your situation?

When a Wife Outearns Her Husband

A LOT of people assume that the permission-to-prosper philosophy is directed only to working wives who earn more than their husbands. Actually, this is only one way that money issues can show up in a dual-career marriage. It's no longer true, as Randi Minetor, author of *Breadwinner Wives*, states, that "men are supposed to bring home the bacon, while the women fry it up in a pan." Society no longer views wives who earn high salaries as aberrations. Since the wife earning more than her husband represents one-third of all marriages now, we'll start with this emotionally charged situation.

Why are there so many wives who earn as much as or more than their husbands today? Chances are you have a friend or colleague who can relate to one of the following reasons: Women are more highly educated now than ever before and are rising in professional stature. Women are prospering in their own businesses. As our lifespan increases, and second and third marriages abound, the chances are higher now that a woman might have a disabled or retired husband while she is still in her prime, with plenty of career ahead of her. With the current volatility of our economy, it is not unusual, unfortunately, for a husband to be out of work. We also know more men who are pursuing passions that satisfy their souls but earn less income, like becoming teachers or clergy or business owners. If husbands are more frequently trading the pursuit of high income for what is deemed as more satisfying work, it is sometimes their wives who pick up the slack in earning household income. Sometimes the wife earns so much more than her husband that it makes sense for him to care for the children while she works.

Let's set the record straight: There are millions of men who are thrilled and delighted that their wives are earning a prosperous living. The more money they earn, the better. The permission-to-prosper issue does not apply to all men—far from it. Melvin is a good example:

For the first fifteen years of our marriage, I made more than my wife. In 1983, she went back to school for a Ph.D. and opened her own practice as a psychologist. She now makes much more than I do. It has never been a problem. It all goes in the same pot, but now the pot is bigger. She always reminds me that my income made it possible for her to go to school and to start her practice. And she still consults with me on financial matters concerning the business. Since her schooling and new job require evening work, I now do all the cooking and shopping, but I enjoy it more than she ever did. She works longer and harder to be a success, and I support her any way I can. Her success doesn't diminish me in any way.

James wanted his wife to be able to take care of herself should he become disabled or die, so he encouraged her to succeed in her own business and regularly assists her in many capacities. For James, his wife's prosperity is reassuring, rather than terrifying. He is confident that she can manage her life if she should have to do so without his financial help.

But even with a country full of Melvins and Jameses, will we as a society ever change so much that a man would feel entitled to the luxury of not having to work by virtue of his agreeing to become someone's "wife"?

I don't think so. That's still the stuff for quirky movies. For all of the evolution we point to with women's careers, I don't believe the tables will ever be turned to the point where men will expect to be rescued financially by their wives. Acceptance of their wives' contributions, maybe, but the term "kept man" is unlikely to enter our societal vocabulary as a common experience. It goes too much against the grain.

Why do some men feel so threatened by a wife who outearns them? The more money a husband earns, the better he may feel about himself as a husband and parent. The more his wife earns, the worse he may feel about himself as a husband and parent. Why the correlation?

It comes down to pride. Fred Hartley, author of *Men and Marriage,* writes:

> Every man has a seed planted deep inside that needs to be nurtured regularly with a sense of dignity. When the respect that dignity requires is not given, something very significant begins to die. For men who are married, the home is designed to be the place where the seed of dignity is nurtured.

And what is undignified about a wife's earning more money than her husband?

Our culture trains men from their earliest adolescent years to aspire to the role of "breadwinner." Just as a woman draws satisfaction from being a good mother, a man's identity and self-esteem are often tied to his success as a provider for those he loves. When a wife helps with (or even takes over) the provider role, her husband's sense of identity may suffer. He isn't sure who he is anymore.

Scott Haltzman, M.D., a psychiatrist specializing in marriage therapy and founder of SecretsofMarriedMen.com, insists:

> When women are the primary providers, they are often robbing their man of his primary identity. It would be the equivalent of having your husband reach over right after you've given birth, pull the baby to his chest, and begin to nurse the baby. As a woman, it's a given that you will nurse the baby or at least have that capability. That's how strongly the majority of men relate to being the provider.

Before we get indignant about how immature their husbands are and how they should learn to grow up, wives must acknowledge how they have helped to create the problem. Some women are not treating their lesser-earning husbands with respect, and the consequences are predictable.

If you earn more than your husband, you can use your greater salary to enhance the life you share with your husband—or you can use it to demean and humiliate him. You may argue with him about his spending habits, because you're earning the money and you don't "approve" of the golf clubs he just purchased. You may pull out your credit card at the restaurant in front of another couple. Or at the beach you may remind your husband that you are both able to have the two-week vacation in the Caribbean only because of your income. Using your earning power to shame your husband will not bring you the happy marriage you desire.

Working wives create trouble in another way. Most women want permission to prosper, but they also want prosperous husbands. Few women actually aspire to be the primary wage earner in the household. You may tolerate it, agree to it, or consider doing it temporarily, but did you dream as a child or adolescent about being the family's provider? For most women, the answer is no. You may find it helpful to acknowledge and resolve your own disappointment if your husband hasn't lived up to your monetary expectations.

What can we learn from the couples where a wife's higher earnings do not cause conflict? What behaviors and attitudes can we emulate?

Some men no longer need to prove their worth to the world. They have matured and realize that real satisfaction does not come from more work and have learned to find just as much validation in the role of husband and father. Work is a way to pay the bills, even a source of real satisfaction, but work is not what excites them about life.

A man's ego can be positively charged, rather than deflated, by his wife's professional status. He can feel like a *cool dude* because someone as amazing as his wife, who is admired by many of her peers, wants to be married to him! He can take pride in watching his wife grow and achieve greatness in her life and in knowing that he helped her get there. He can feel proud of his wife's accomplishments, because there is such a pervasive sense of "we-ness" in the marriage that there is no need to separate what her accomplishments are and what theirs are together. What's good for her is good not only *for* him but also *because* of him, and she lets him know it.

In marriages where men are at peace with their prosperous wives, women take care to frequently let their husbands know how valued they are. They don't rub the money imbalance into his face to make themselves feel more important. They might even be sensitive and generous enough to allow their husbands to pay for dinner in a restaurant in front of another couple, even though both of them know that the money for that bill comes mostly from her paycheck.

A wise wife learns to reassure her husband frequently that he is an essential partner to her and that she couldn't flourish without him. She thanks him often and tells her friends what an incredible husband she has. She gives him public, as well as private, accolades. She shows interest in his career and hobbies, even if they bring in less money. She does not evaluate her husband's worth by what he earns. Each partner in this marriage genuinely wants the other to be happy and prosperous, and rather than concentrate on what the wife's career takes away from them, they focus on what it adds to their lives.

Sometimes a husband comes to see the benefits of being married to a breadwinner wife, even if it scared him initially. When there is more money in the house, the financial pressure on him is lightened, his wife is happier and a more interesting person to be around, and he can spend more meaningful time with family, personal hobbies, religious studies, and community. Eventually, his grumpiness may turn to gratitude, so much so that he will even discourage her from leaving her high-paying career if it means that he would have to give up some of the perks.

Even if outside influences raise eyebrows at your having chosen to marry a man who makes less than you, more and more women like Cheryl are discovering that what matters most is whether you married a good guy who really cares about you:

> I have felt some flak from friends who think that my significant other is not "good enough" for me because of the differences in our education. I have two professional degrees, and my husband is a high school–educated welder. How much money a man earns is not important to me, so long as he has financial integrity. If he pays his bills on time, keeps a slush fund for emergencies, and keeps his debts down, then that's great for me! The more educated men that I dated tended to be way over their heads in debt. Better pay means better living standards, which equates to higher debt. No, thank you! I'm so grateful I didn't pass by my loving, generous husband!

When Your Husband Is Disabled or Retired

JEFFREY WAS not resistant when his wife's business started to earn money—he was thrilled. He has no problem with her becoming a multimillionaire:

> I can think of a thousand things I'd rather do than work for a living. My worth as a human being is in no way tied up in how much money I make. I don't want to leave a billion dollars to charity or our kids. I'm not driven to make a million dollars a year. I hate being bossed around, so I don't like to report for a job. I like doing what I want. If she figures out a way with her own business to bring a ton of money into the house, I'll quit my job and retire. Sounds great to me!

Sometimes a woman's husband not only earns less than she does; he actually earns next to nothing. He may have become disabled. He may have been downsized or fired and become unemployable. He may have retired with a small pension or decided to pursue a new passion in his life, like becoming a baseball coach or a high school teacher. In any case, the burden of providing for a family now rests more significantly on his wife's shoulders.

To show you how embedded our societal norm of the male provider is, what image comes to your mind if I say, "My wife doesn't work"? You probably think that she is either a full-time mother or married to a successful man so she doesn't "have to work." Now, what image pops up if someone says to you, "My husband doesn't work"? Do you immediately assume that he is taking care of children or that he is married to a wealthy woman who affords him the luxury of

endless days of golf? Only if you are told so. *We are programmed to think of women who don't work as lucky and of men
who don't work as weird.*

Women don't always choose the breadwinner role. Sometimes life foists it upon them, and they rise to the occasion.
How this goes over with a husband has everything to do with
how he feels about the reason he stopped working. If he did
so of his own volition (like retirement), with his self-esteem
high, he will become her biggest fan. He can focus his energies on helping her instead of on building his own career, and
he can help pick up some of the workload at home. He is also
emotionally available to her as a confidant and friend, because
he is not so distracted by worries about his own work.

He has "been there, done that," so when she comes home
bone tired or worried about a perplexing employee issue, he
often knows exactly how she feels. This man doesn't feel intimidated by his wife's earnings, because he does not identify
his lack of work as a failure.

The man who stops working because his body failed him
or a company let him down can be a whole different story. His
ego is already bruised enough without having salt rubbed in
the wound. Now his wife has to take care of him? How humiliating! He can easily become tyrannical or depressed as he
sorts through his pain and tries to accept a new relationship
between him and his wife.

This kind of transition will either break a marriage or
make it stronger. A man may need to work through depression, anger, and acceptance of his losses. Dr. Haltzman remarks: "Like the cat who proudly displays a mouse, laying it
down at the feet of the homeowner, many men bring home
their paycheck as a way of showing that they are making a

contribution to the success of the household. It may be symbolic, but it is an important exchange of currency." The loss of that currency can leave a man feeling not only broke, but also broken. But take heart. Time does heal many wounds. He may slowly begin to accept his wife's burgeoning career and then to support and even applaud it—but only if she can convince him that she is not going to leave him. He needs to know that his wife still needs him—if not as a financial supporter, then as a soul mate, lover, and friend.

What can you do if you are married to a nonworking man who is sensitive about being supported by his wife?

First, give it time, a year or two or even longer. If you judge your husband by his initial reaction to his setback, you could be giving up on a relationship that still has much to offer once he heals from his grief. It can be helpful to get professional counseling. You may feel real anger and disappointment at your husband for having let you down or forced you into a role you didn't ask for, even if it wasn't his fault. You can manage any anger and resentment, but only if you make the effort to do so; otherwise, they can poison even the closest of relationships.

Second, say thank you to your husband at every opportunity—he needs to feel valued by you. Be grateful for your work, which will give you a positive focus outside of the home and a place to escape to when you need an emotional break from the pressures of your marriage and your husband's troubles. Say thank you for the small and big blessings of your life, which you might take for granted when you are consumed with trauma. Say thanks to God that it isn't any worse; it could always be worse. A grateful heart goes a long way toward healing stress in a marriage.

When You Earn Your Own Money for the First Time

ANOTHER CRITICAL transition in the life of a dual-career couple is the time that the wife starts developing her own career, usually after having been a stay-at-home mom for a number of years. The woman can approach this decision with a widely fluctuating attitude toward her husband.

Sometimes a woman resents her husband's inability to support the household alone and grieves because she cannot be at home with her children. She is working only because she has to, and she isn't happy about it. She may take out her resentment on her husband, who may in turn feel persecuted for his inadequacy as a provider.

> The idea that a woman would give up work upon marriage—the assumption being that wifehood is a full-time job—now seems as quaint as ironing tea towels, or beating rugs with a stick.
>
> —Susan Maushart, *Wifework*

A full-time stay-at-home wife is a symbol of career success for a man. When she goes to work, both of them can feel disappointed or even devastated by this "evidence" that the family can no longer afford for her to stay home. Other women go to work before their children are grown because they want to learn and work in a field that interests them.

Do not underestimate the seismic tremor that occurs in a marriage when a wife starts earning her own money for the first time. Perhaps she received an "allowance" to spend for household and personal items, and now she gets her own paycheck. She may have previously deferred to her husband on all financial management issues; now she expects to offer more input.

I N MOST relationships where a woman has previously sur-rendered money management and investment decisions to her partner, any attempt to change this pattern is bound to shake things up. Initially, the partner may feel threatened by a request to give up some of his power in making major finan-cial decisions. But once he weathers the storm of watching the relationship change in a way that is out of his control, he often experiences a profound sense of relief at no longer hav-ing to carry all the responsibility by himself.

—Olivia Mellan, *Money Shy to Money Sure*

A woman's new commitment to work will usually change the way the family handles financial management. Will she open up her own checking account, or will all of her new in-come go directly into the family's joint account? If she's start-ing a business of her own, how much of her income will go toward the business versus paying the family's bills? How much discretionary money can she spend without her hus-band's permission?

Will the family now, for the first time, define money as "his money" and "her money"? Again, attitude is everything. Even if they have separate checking accounts and each spouse is allowed a certain amount of discretionary personal spending, if both see their earnings as "our money" and the goal as creating what the family needs, there will be less stress on the marriage. If a wife is working only to pay the bills and she would quit in a heartbeat if the money weren't needed, it is unlikely that she will fight for independent money and financial management. (It's also unlikely that she will seriously crave permission to prosper.) But if she is pursuing work out of personal desire rather than financial need and her husband isn't crazy about her working, suddenly her wanting to open a separate checking account takes on a whole new meaning, especially for her husband.

Separate accounts may make the husband worry about secrets. Is she going to be forthright with him about her income? He used to be totally in control of the money in his wife's pocket, and now he isn't. If the marriage is troubled, is she building up a safety net so that she can leave him? To him, separate money could symbolize a failed marriage.

The fights in the marriage may be about money, but they could camouflage the real issue. Perhaps this husband misses his wife, or she is attracted to someone at the office; perhaps she used to spend more time with the children, and now, with her home less often, they're acting out, which raises the stress level in the house. He may be hurt because he believes she loves her work more than time with him. He feels like he is in competition with her work now—and men do not like competition unless they can win. To him, winning might mean getting his wife to quit her job or reduce her hours, but to her, winning means doubling her income and getting a promotion.

In this case, what looks like a fight about money is really two exhausted and lonely parents taking out their frustrations on each other.

Listen for a moment to Kathy. Kathy is a high earner married to a professional whose income fluctuates wildly. She believes that it just doesn't work for a woman to be financially supported by her husband:

An equal and loving, supportive relationship, where two people love and adore each other, needs to be built on respect, trust, and faith in each other. This does not allow for one person to not earn and share in the financial burden. I truly believe that men respect women who work. I have never had a man put me down for working or for being successful. The truth is they call me at home and ask me to help their wives.

I agree with half of Kathy's statement but not with the other half. She's right—having respect, trust, and faith in each other is essential, and many men do respect their wives for working. What's not true is that it can never work to have a marriage of unequal earners. You and your husband will not earn the same amount of money for year after year of your marriage. Over the history of your marriage, one of you will usually be making more than the other, sometimes substantially more, and the roles can switch back and forth.

As discussed earlier, in the marital relationship money is not only the currency you bring to the supermarket but also the symbolic representation of power. Given that, when a wife first starts earning her own money, ideally two things will happen simultaneously: The first is that her husband will greet her new earnings with applause and gratitude, and he'll work on his own issues and insecurities without dumping all over her (or at least in honest communication with her and a therapist if necessary). The second is that she will make it clear from the beginning that she is delighted about her new income because of how it can strengthen their life together, not just her life alone.

Finally, communication, communication, communication. Did I say communication? When both he and she have been used to her being at home, taking care of all the meals and parenting and spending only what her husband made, her evolution to a working wife is a really big deal. Her first job outside of the house is more than a new career; it represents an upheaval in the household, albeit for wonderful reasons. The new situation should be treated with respect and appropriate concern until all are used to their new roles, much as you would expect when the first baby is born into the household.

When the Wife Earns Too Little Money

WHILE SOME husbands try to stop their wives from working, others go beyond encouraging a wife's prosperity—they demand it. The source of money tension in the marriage is not that she is earning money but that she isn't earning enough. (We women are getting a taste of our own medicine.) He's tired of supporting her Ph.D. program, or he thinks it's time for her to work part-time so that he doesn't have to work overtime. If she hasn't proven herself to be profitable according to his standards, he might view her new business as a hobby and pressure her to close it down just when she is looking to him for emotional support.

Some men view their wives' new fledgling business as Jim does: "It's so rewarding for me to see someone I care about becoming excited and happy in her work." But other husbands, like Delmae's, are frustrated by the sacrifices they must make to compensate for their wives' lack of earnings. Delmae says:

For the past three years, I have been working full-time in network marketing, making decent income (still working on my first million!). Almost a week doesn't go by without my husband's asking, begging, or demanding that I go get a "real" job. He believes that my lack of income "forces" him to stay in a job he dislikes, which seems to me to be his issue and not mine. He's also resentful that I love what I do; I work from home and have time and freedom that he feels he can't have.

Delmae and her husband have come to believe that only one of them at a time can have an enjoyable and prosperous job. They are competing with each other for that right, instead of figuring out how both of them can create what they want.

Your husband is most likely to see your work as a "hobby" when you are just getting started or if your low income continues beyond expectations of when it would rise. He may feel impatient for you to start sharing the burden of earning household income, perhaps because he's unhappy with his own career or earning power or because a milestone is approaching, like a child entering college.

It may take patience and perseverance to overcome your husband's resistance to your new career. Of course, success helps, too. When your husband can't or won't be your cheerleader and in fact is often the guy who starts making you question your ability to pull it off, put together your own cheerleading team of girlfriends, supportive family members, and business colleagues who will hang in there with you until you can sweetly whisper in your husband's ear, "I told you I'd do it," as you dine in a five-star restaurant on your company's credit card.

Seven Rules for Discussing Money—or Any Other Hot Topic

FOLLOWING ARE seven universal strategies for more effective communication about money issues in your marriage, regardless of their source.

1. *Timing is essential.* Most couples fight about money right at the moment when a hot button is pushed, when one of them is running out the door or trying to sleep, or when the kids are screaming for attention. Treat money as if it were a sensitive sexual problem. Would you talk about it in front of the kids? Would you bring it up when your husband, briefcase in hand, is headed out the door?

Money fights are inflammatory. Don't discuss a money problem when one of you is angry or is closing the car door, late for work. Don't hit your spouse with money complaints five minutes after he gets home from the office. The next time you are about to open your mouth to complain about a money issue, ask yourself if this is a moment you would choose to discuss your sexual relationship with your husband. If either of you is tired, if you don't have privacy, or if you're not fully awake, save it for later.

2. *If you don't deal with the fear, you'll get nowhere.* Here is a common scenario: He wants to clean out the savings account and go $10,000 into debt to finance a new business, but she's terrified when the savings account gets below $20,000, and she hates credit card debt. How will they find a happy medium?

By identifying her "intolerables." Maybe she would like $20,000 in the checking account, but she'd find less than $5,000 intolerable. Maybe she'd prefer that they cut up all their credit cards, but she can live with a balance of less than two grand. Her husband must address her real fear ("I'm afraid that you'll wipe us out and we'll be living on the street with a shopping cart"), or she'll try to put the brakes on the business just to be sure that her intolerable, worst-case-scenario disaster doesn't happen.

When tempers are flaring around money, you can bet that fear is lurking behind the anger. Resolve that fear, and money discussions and negotiations become much easier.

3. *Beware of teasing.* It usually backfires on you if you mock your spouse about "love handles," bad breath, or money. Shelley, a high-earning wife, admits, "Sometimes I tease my husband and say, 'I'm going to go have lunch with my Fortune 500 account now,' and he'll tease back with 'If you close the deal, I might let you have sex with me tonight.'" Shelley knows she can tease her husband about money—it doesn't upset him. But he is rare.

You have to know your spouse's sensitivities and whether he enjoys being teased. If it really hurts him, curb the reflex. Some spouses are too insecure or unskilled to address resentments in their marriage directly, so they do it through teasing and sarcastic remarks. This only inflames the tension.

If you notice that sarcastic remarks have started to slip too easily off your tongue, it's a clue that you and your partner have some talking to do; there's something bothering you that you aren't dealing with in an up-front way. Gentleness goes over better than righteous anger, and simply asking for what you want works better than sarcastic teasing.

4. *Avoid the actual words "We have to talk."* Okay, so you know you have to talk. But every man seems to be wired to shut down or go into defense mode immediately upon hearing those four words. He can't even hear what you have to say, because as soon as you've said the words, he's already the defense lawyer building a case for his innocence.

Instead, say something along these lines: "I'd like to feel closer to you than we've been this past week. Can we set aside a few moments to connect tonight after the kids go to sleep?"

5. *Try not talking about it.* You may think that talking things out is the answer to every problem in your marriage. Sometimes, talking is what you need but the last thing your husband needs. Balance is the key. Some money problems come from basic differences in your personality, and you are better off working on your own attitude than hashing it out one more time.

For example, let's say it really bugs you when your husband pays the bills late. He has a lackadaisical attitude to the problem ("They're charging us too much money anyway; let them wait!"), and no matter how much you talk about it, the problem hasn't been resolved in the past three years.

Instead of another repetitive fight where you attack his character and bad money habits and he defends himself, try an alternative. Tell him that you've been thinking about how paying the bills doesn't seem to be well-suited to his personality, so starting next month, you'll be paying all the bills. Thank him for all of his efforts thus far, and let him know that he's welcome to object but that you are no longer willing to stick with your old approach unless he commits to paying the bills on time. Don't deliver the message in an angry way or demand another drawn-out discussion about it. You've reached your limit of tolerance, and you are creating a solution. Tell him if he wants to talk about it, you are available; otherwise, the new arrangement will begin the following month.

Another alternative is to do the opposite—bite your tongue and learn to live with a few late bills. Let him know that you've decided to leave him alone about paying the bills, as long as he doesn't go a full thirty days or risk losing the mortgage, your health insurance, or the electricity (or whatever is on your intolerable list). No more negotiations or attacks on his character. Learn to live with the fact that your husband doesn't pay bills the way you would, but what he's doing is not worth fighting about anymore.

6. *Take a time-out.* Money talks often have a lot of energy to them. A conversation can quickly escalate into a fight, which can become so heated that each of you starts saying hurtful things to the other and nothing is accomplished but polarization. Call for a time-out when your fight is spinning out of control, but not in the usual way a couple does this. What's typical? One of you slams the door, says something nasty, and stomps out of the room. You've achieved your time-out, but at what price? Instead, calmly say something like, "We are about to say some really hurtful things to each other. Let's take ten minutes (or half an hour, or whatever you think will work) to calm down, and then resume this conversation."

You might fear that the problem will never be resolved if you don't take care of it immediately, but once you have moved from discussion to fighting, it won't get resolved anyway.

7. *Empathize with your partner's position whenever possible.* You don't have to agree with your partner's point of view in order to express empathy, which will dramatically decrease your partner's resistance and anger. Let's say that your husband is angry because you have insisted that you want your own checking account for discretionary spending, after having had a joint account for twenty years of marriage. He is understandably threatened and angry, although you feel completely entitled and don't want to give in to his demands that you not open the account.

Instead of accusing him of being a jerk for giving you a hard time, try this approach: "I understand why this is a problem for you, and I bet if I were in your shoes, I'd feel the same way. I know that getting my own checking account really bothers you, and I'm sorry about that. This is something I need to do for myself. I just want you to know that I love you, and I have no intention of hurting you. If there is a way that you could feel better about my having my own account, please tell me what that is, because I really don't want you to be upset."

Honoring your spouse's feelings, and validating that he has a right to those feelings, is not the same as agreeing that his position is right. Nor do you have to give up what you want to do. You can stand up for yourself—but with respect and consideration for how your actions affect your beloved.

Giving Yourself Permission to Prosper

NO CHAPTER on resolving money conflicts related to your career would be complete without reminding you that often it's not your husband's permission to prosper you need but your own.

I can be very persuasive, and my husband is very easygoing. I've learned that when he really has a strongly held opinion, even though I probably could talk him over to my point of view, I don't do it. I get my way so much that it's best to let him be right when it really matters to him. This gives us a better balance in our relationship. I didn't understand that when I was married before. Back then, I thought it was my job to get my way every time.

—Denise

As tempting as it is to lay blame, working wives usually have trouble prospering in their careers because of internal conflicts, not a problem husband. They are caught between wanting to prosper and wanting to be taken care of, afraid that if they become too successful, their husbands won't want to be married to them anymore.

You might be married to a great guy who has even agreed to be a full-time stay-at-home dad, and he's amazing at taking care of the house. You are free to pursue your career with abandon. But you miss your kids, and you are uncomfortable about handing over all of the "woman's work" to your husband. Dean responded this way to my research:

My wife is the breadwinner, as I elected to stay home to raise our daughter. I am usually self-employed, and it was my choice to devote this time to the family. When our daughter was eighteen months old, I became a licensed home day care provider to bring other children into the home to interact with our daughter. I earned about $500 per week doing this.

It intrigues me that women might hold themselves back because of a need to remain in place in the antique hierarchy of breadwinning. I have noticed my wife's income has plateaued, although in her field her income should be rising each year.

Your ambivalence about prosperity could cause you to unconsciously sabotage your work so that a promotion passes you by. You might work fewer hours than your peers, because you are ambivalent about giving up precious time with your family. You may justify to yourself taking a lesser-paying or less stressful job because of your so-called incompetent or unsupportive husband, when he never demanded any such thing. Your conflicts about success may be rooted in your own lack of confidence or self-worth; if you've got a great family and work you love, and the money is rolling in, too, a part of you may feel unworthy of such a blessing.

As one woman revealed in my research, "It has taken me a long time to allow myself to be the real me and to accept that I deserve it all, because I've worked hard for it and I've earned it!"

Other books have addressed a woman's fear of success and what you can do about it. This book is aimed specifically at marital issues related to permission to prosper. Before you assume that your money problems are the fault of the man you married, look in the mirror and delve deeply into your own psyche. Your own attitudes and choices are within your power to change.

CHAPTER SIX

Children and Stress

I MARRIED MY husband, Stephen, when he had custody of his two boys from a former marriage, then ages ten and fourteen. The only honeymoon we took was a short getaway for a couple of days while the boys stayed with his ex-wife. When we returned home, I was an instant parent. Shortly after we were married, I became pregnant with our first daughter, Sarah, and within the next four years, her two siblings joined her. Becoming "Mrs. Jaffe" brought a husband and children all at once, so for me "wife" and "mother" have been intertwined since our courtship.

Although combining a career with parenting as I did is increasingly common in second marriages, it isn't like that for thousands of women who delay having children until their thirties and forties. Many choose not to have children because of career pressures, out of a feeling that they "aren't ready," or because they haven't found the right man to marry and raise children with. Gone are the days when hopeful grandparents-to-be would worry if a newlywed couple didn't announce a child on the way within the first year of marriage. Marriage and motherhood do not necessarily go hand in hand.

Sylvia Ann Hewlett created a stir in spring 2002 with her book *Creating a Life: Professional Women and the Quest for Children,* based on a national survey of 1,186 high-achieving career women, ages twenty-eight to fifty-five, who were either employed full-time or self-employed. Her research tells a troubling story:

> Unwanted childlessness haunts the executive suite. A number of factors might be at play. The time was never right. Marriages failed. Potential husbands with big egos did not want to marry a hard-charging woman earning big money. Career ambitions intervened, and promotions were hard to come by if the boss detected baby hunger.

Hewlett found:

- 33 percent of these high-achieving women were childless at forty.
- 42 percent of all the women surveyed were childless.
- 49 percent of ultra-achievers—those earning more than $100,000 per year—were childless.
- 25 percent of childless high achievers ages forty-one to fifty-five would have still liked to have had a child.
- 31 percent of older ultra-achievers still wanted a child.
- Overall, only 11–14 percent of those without children preferred it that way.

Research like Hewlett's (and that contained in Peggy Orenstein's *Flux*) confirms that many women who are childless later in life didn't really plan to be; many regret having put their careers first or not having found the right partner at the right time. In the past decade, the number of U.S. mothers giving birth after forty has nearly doubled, to more than 94,000 in 2000. Los Angeles gynecologist and author Judith Reichman, M.D., says, "Women are suddenly realizing, at forty, 'Oh, my God, I forgot to have a baby!'"

But what about those couples who didn't "forget" to get pregnant but actually planned to be childless? It's time we let women and men off the hook when they make a clear, calm decision to devote their energies to work rather than to raising children. If a woman cannot have children because of infertility, she earns sympathy. If she chooses not to raise children because of an all-consuming commitment to career, she is often viewed as self-centered and shallow.

What if a woman's mission in life is career-oriented—and the next cure for breast cancer will come from a woman who couldn't or didn't have children but instead devoted fifteen-hour workdays to the relentless pursuit of a cure for cancer? But a woman doesn't have to discover the cure for cancer to justify a personal choice to devote her life energy to her career rather than to parenting.

> If a married couple with children has fifteen minutes of uninterrupted, nonlogistical, non-problem-solving talk every day, I would put them in the top 5 percent of all married couples in the land. It's an extraordinary achievement.
>
> —William J. Doherty, Ph.D., *Take Back Your Marriage*

Each couple must face this sensitive and complicated issue head-on and make the best decision they can. Many a woman has resisted her husband's pressure to begin a family, negotiating to wait "until my next promotion," only to find out that fertility isn't so easy once she feels that she is ready.

Many a man has pleaded with his wife to work full-time after the other children have entered school full-time, but she begs for "one more baby." He's insists, "We can barely afford to take care of the children we already have!"

Deciding whether or not to have a child is an issue that is well beyond the scope of this book, but here are four guidelines that may help you and your husband approach this subject together:

1. Discuss the topic respectfully and calmly, instead of resorting to fighting, name-calling, and throwing out ultimatums. Often, clergy or a trained marriage counselor can be helpful. Family and friends may not be, because they may have a biased opinion about what the couple should do.

2. Realize that every marriage requires compromise and that there may be no solution that will be perfect for both parties. It may come down to doing what one wants and what the other can learn to live with.

3. Refrain from attacks on character ("You are a self-centered workaholic, just like your dad"); value judgments ("God said, 'Be fruitful and multiply,' so you can't call yourself a religious person if you don't want to have another baby!"); and pessimistic, exaggerated accusations ("You never think about anyone but yourself!").

4. Start with what you share in common, instead of focusing on the differences, and from there brainstorm a solution that makes sense to both of you. For example, maybe you agree that raising a child could be meaningful, but you

don't want to jeopardize your career status by becoming pregnant and then working part-time for several months of leave. The option of becoming foster parents might be a satisfying solution, but you'll never have this conversation if you are always focused on your reluctance to get pregnant and your husband's negative judgments about a life without children.

If you don't have (or don't plan to have) children, you can skip ahead to the next chapter. But if children are a part of your life, keep reading.

Now That They're Here: Dealing with the Emotional Pressures of Parenting

NO MATTER how much you love them, children are a lot of work. When both a husband and wife are stretched emotionally and physically by the demands of child rearing and two careers, tensions naturally mount in a marriage. Exhaustion becomes a constant companion. There just aren't enough hours in the day to devote to two busy careers, the demands of raising children, community service and religious worship, physical fitness, leisure time, extended family, and then—oh, yes, don't forget—sustaining an intimate marriage.

It's easy to blame children for the increasing distance between spouses (more on this topic in chapter 7): "If only we weren't so tired and overcommitted, we'd have so much more romance in our life together" or "If both of us weren't so involved in our careers, maybe we wouldn't be fighting so much." It was easier when the father's career always came first and the mother followed without argument. Now she expects an equal vote!

It's not unusual for even the most loving working mom to have mixed emotions about parenthood. Do any of the following questions sound familiar?

- Did I do the right thing by putting my baby into child care when he was three months old?
- Would I have been able to build a successful practice if I hadn't cut back to part-time for three years?
- Parenting doesn't seem very rewarding when my child is whining all the time. Would I feel more appreciated if I spent more time at work?
- I just can't lose the fifty pounds I put on during my last pregnancy. Will I ever fit into my business suits again?
- Do I really want a nanny raising my child? Should I do the unthinkable and walk away from my six-figure job to stay at home and raise her myself?
- Did I marry the right guy? He didn't turn out to be the provider I imagined he'd be. If he earned more money, I could stay home with my children like I always wanted to do.

The questions are endless, because opportunities for women have expanded so greatly. With so many choices come much second-guessing and angst. Now unhappy mothers perceive that they have a viable alternative to parenting that offers meaning: "If I weren't spending my time dealing with kids, I could be earning money and enjoying a rewarding and stimulating career instead." Millions of women love the work that they do but remain susceptible to the centuries-old belief that being a mother should always come first. Women are more comfortable saying that they work "because they have to pay the bills" than what's true for many—they work because they love working.

Not only is a wife automatically supposed to want to be a mother, but once she has achieved this biological feat, she's also supposed to love it. Many successful working mothers harbor a secret that they cringe to admit: They love their children and are grateful for their presence, but they find it difficult to be at home all day with children. Their careers are rewarding to them in a way that parenting is not. Pat, a busy professional married to a stay-at-home dad, honestly shares this:

> I feel guilty about wanting to work, rather than stay at home with kids. I've felt that all my life, looking at my mother who stayed home, raising eight kids, and all I could think of was, "I don't want that." It looked too hard; she looked tired all the time. Aside from my husband, no one loves my kids more than I do. But I would go crazy being at home with them. My husband is a very energetic, creative force who thinks nothing of taking the entire troupe out to a park to fly a kite. He remembers what it's like to be a kid. My guilt stems from not being the perfect, doting mother who records her child's every breath.

Pat has a husband who is home full-time with the children and whom she feels very confident about, but many working wives don't have that comfort. Ambivalence about career success and prosperity arises for a mother when she is unavailable to children who need her. The question for the mother is, When can my child live without my presence? Perhaps she can't bear to give up nursing, but she makes peace with missing her son's football games. Some working mothers don't give themselves permission to fully pursue a career until the children are grown and out of the house.

Other women struggle all of their working lives with the sacrifices in family life that they make to honor their devotion to their career. Scarcely ever does it become okay for a wife to admit to herself, or others, that she "selfishly" put her own satisfaction before that of her children. Most such women can't bear to admit that they work just because it feels good to do so.

How a woman balances her commitments to work and family—and how she resolves these issues with her husband—has a strong bearing on whether or not she receives her husband's permission to prosper. As we explore creating an egalitarian home with an equally involved father, we must remember that a woman's internal conflict about loving her work and her children will directly influence how she either encourages or sabotages a more involved husband. Some working moms can never come to peace with their own guilt about having given up the primary caregiver role; their husbands can't win, because if the men step forward with willingness and ability, their wives criticize them until they retreat. It is too threatening (and too guilt provoking) when their husbands take over the caregiver role.

Other wives are unapologetic about their career commitments, believing strongly that they are better mothers because of it, so they eagerly seek men who will help share the workload at home.

Men have always been able to equate their ability to provide financial resources for a family with being a good parent. For women, the issue is more complex. Still, it is hard to argue with the fact that a woman who is fulfilled, enthusiastic, healthy, successful, and contented is far more likely to be a loving and effective parent than one who is resentful, bitter, bored, or frustrated. Whether or not you are a parent is not the issue; your contentment with your choice is.

IN SEARCH OF THE ELUSIVE EGALITARIAN FATHER

What image comes to mind when you imagine the ideal egalitarian father? If you're like most women, you probably envision a fifty-fifty division of labor. If I change the baby's diaper before dinner, you do the next one. If I give the kids a bath on Tuesday, you do it on Thursday. If I run Johnny to soccer and karate, you take care of getting Suzanne to basketball and hockey. I get one night off a week to go out with the girls, and you take another night to hang with your friends. You understand that my career is as demanding as yours is, so you don't expect me to do child care more than half of the time. It's only fair!

What's wrong with this picture?

First, you must define "equal." Is it hours spent or the number of times the task must be repeated? If the family requires seven dinners a week, for it to be equal must you eat out as a family one night a week and then have each spouse cook three dinners a week? If you spend two hours with the kids after school, must your spouse spend two hours with them in the evening for it to be "fair"?

> Being equals does not mean being or doing the same things. It means that each spouse feels valued and believes that he or she has choices.
>
> —Michael Obsatz, *From Stalemate to Soulmate*

At the root of the fairness issue are two fears:

1. You will not be respected and valued.
2. Your own needs will not be met.

If a husband expected his wife to do all of the housework because "it's women's work" and he communicated the feeling that his career is more important than hers, she would likely feel devalued and disrespected as a human being. Then she would see the hours she spends on household responsibilities, compared with what he spends, as a comment on what her time is worth.

This attitude can set up in a marriage a weird dynamic where the spouses actually compete with each other over whose career requires more hours (thus is more respected and important). In such a case, the children (who have two distracted, absentee parents) are the ultimate losers.

The primary issue is not getting time to lie in bed and watch soap operas while your husband watches the kids; it's having the time and energy to prosper—to work hard, keep customers happy, achieve recognition from peers, earn promotions, and pursue excellence. Many working mothers fear that the time they devote to caring for children is time they "should" be spending on the job.

The *details* of how a husband and wife share parenting responsibilities are not as important as ensuring that both feel respected and that the needs of both are being met. You must recognize when, as we discussed earlier, your so-called equal partnership begins to deteriorate into an obsession with score keeping.

It reminds me of a scene I recently experienced with my daughters, Sarah and Elana. I had set up a reward system for each girl, to help each break a bad habit that needed some "redirection." Each girl was to get her own reward for breaking her own, unique habit.

Elana, age six, piped up with, "But Mommy, that's not fair. I don't do (what Sarah does), so I should get the prize she's getting, too!" In Elana's thinking, Sarah got a reward for not doing *x,* so if Elana didn't do *x,* she should get the same reward. Ah, yes, the god of fairness had come for another visit.

Release yourself from using the yardstick of fairness, and you will more easily accept what the research shows: The man who will truly share child-rearing responsibilities with his wife fifty-fifty is about one out of ten at best, unless she is the family's sole wage earner and he is home full-time with the kids. Here's what's more likely.

Even if a husband does half of the work (and that's rare), his wife does most of the planning. She keeps track of the birthday parties, special events at school, when book order money is collected, and when Jessica has to be picked up for late rehearsals at school for the school play. The husband might pick up Jessica, but his wife will tell him that it needs to be done. He runs errands for the house, but his wife gives him the list.

He might spend as much time with the children as she does—thereby meeting the criterion of equal parenting time—but some men prefer to choose how they spend their time and will do only what they feel like. They may insist on remaining in control of their schedules and how they use their limited time outside of work. Many husbands are most comfortable doing fun stuff with the kids, leaving to their wives some of the more unpleasant tasks, like homework and baths.

Maybe you put the younger kids to bed every night, which is something you mostly enjoy, but your husband takes your fourteen-year-old son on his paper route. All totaled, it takes you twice as long to do the bedtime routine, but you'd just as soon not get up at five in the morning for the paper route. Perhaps you are the primary caregiver for the children after school and most evenings, but that's okay for you as long as your husband is always available on Thursday evenings so that you can go to your bible study group. You don't really need him to spend equal time with the kids—what you really need is to be guilt-free about taking off for your Thursday-night class. Truthfully, if he, instead of you, were watching the kids half the week, it wouldn't sit right with you as a mother.

You and your husband will be a lot happier when you let go of measuring your marital satisfaction with a stopwatch, worrying less about getting what you "deserve," and focusing more on how to get what you really need.

When you are deciding who should do what regarding parenting responsibilities, consider the effort required for the task. Reading my children a bedtime story energizes me; I bounce back up from the job and often return to my computer for work or to household responsibilities. On the other hand, when my husband reads to them, he is lulled to sleep by the activity. On many occasions the children have giggled as Daddy snored halfway through their story. So unless my husband wants to go to sleep at eight o'clock, I put the children to bed. And that's okay with both of us.

Maybe you think you want an equally involved husband, when what you really need is one night off from taking care of kids. Or you complain that your husband never cooks, but what you really want is his blessing for take-out pizza one night a week, or you want to walk away from the table when dinner is over and let him deal with dirty dishes. You think you need a husband who wants to spend time with the kids the way you do, but what you really want is a husband who is willing to step in and give you a break when you are feeling burned-out.

Maybe if you got what you *thought* you needed—a husband who is as involved in parenting as you are—you'd actually feel conflicted. It's not equal time you need so much as a husband who is there for you, in attitude and action, when you need it.

Women have spent many hours kvetching about the disparity between their husbands' parenting activity and their own, dreaming of some help to relieve the burden of constant demands on their schedule and their energy. Our husbands today are far more involved than our fathers were, so we are moving in the right direction, but how can you convince your husband to be more involved if it's not enough?

First of all, silence the little voice that cries out with resentment, "They're his kids, too. I shouldn't have to beg him to spend time with them. He should want to, because he's their father!"

"Shoulding" your husband only drives him further away. Who are his role models for involved parenting? His own father? Your husband may want to be more active, but men often are not the multitaskers women are; when their headspace is devoted to earning a living, many of them have trouble shifting into parenting mode. Women can wipe a runny nose and help a child get a snack while cooking dinner and talking to a client on the phone. Men often don't operate that way, so when we ask our husbands to be more involved in parenting, they have to be willing to set aside other obligations to give the children their full focus.

Like it or not, you may also have to teach your husband to do the things you take for granted (like caring for sick children or playing dress-up), not because he's incompetent or uncaring but because these tasks are unlikely to be part of his life experience thus far. This sort of "training" is best accomplished with warmth, appreciation, and genuine respect.

Unfortunately many women feel bitter about unmet expectations. Somewhere they got the idea that women's rights in the workplace would translate into women's rights in the home and that men would learn how to be active parents simply because it's the right thing to do now that their wives are working. Many husbands are happy to let their wives deal with parenting unless they are asked to help and told specifically what to do—just as many wives naturally expect their husbands to mow the lawn and change the oil in the car.

Try to let go of your demand that your husband be as involved with the children as you are, and get clear with him about what you really need. Let's say you want to move your husband from 20 percent contribution to 40. Here's how to invite his active participation in parenting:

- Select child-care tasks that are within his ability, helpful to you, and good for the kids.
- Thank him for contributing, even if you think he's only doing what he's supposed to be doing.
- Help him see the benefits to you of giving you a break, which ultimately come back to him in the form

of a more affectionate, more easygoing, and sexier wife.

▪ Encourage his involvement with the kids in fun activities that have their own rewards, so that he comes to love parenting instead of seeing it as added items on his to-do list.

▪ Don't expect as much multitasking from him as you— his brain isn't wired that way. He'll be careless, distracted, frustrated, and overwhelmed in no time if you ask him to juggle five tasks simultaneously the way you easily do, unless you happen to have married the rare man with that gift.

▪ If you expect a parenting task from him and he demonstrates that he's either no good at it or is not committed to doing it the way you think he should be, find him something else to do. Then either do the job yourself or outsource it.

▪ Beware of sending mixed messages. Don't tell him you want him to be more involved with the children and then insist on your being in charge. He is not your *nanny;* he is your *partner.*

▪ Love does not mean never having to ask. Don't wait until you are a screaming maniac to ask for your husband's help. Ask him to pitch in while you are still calm, so he doesn't hear a shrieking demand that makes him want to give you less, not more.

▪ Rave about your husband as a father, both in private and in public. When you make him feel good about being a great dad, he'll be inspired to live up to your perception of him. If all you do is complain about him, in front of him and to others, he'll live up to that expectation, too.

Dealing with an Incompetent or Unwilling Dad

PERHAPS YOU'VE tried every strategy that I've mentioned above, and more, but you are confronting the truth about who you married. He's a good guy, but an involved father he'll never be. He's too old-fashioned or too stubborn, too unskilled, too much of a workaholic, too short-tempered, too old, too sick—well, you get the picture. This guy just isn't going to change much, and since you don't plan on leaving him, you'll have to learn to be a "single parent." What should you do?

When you need your husband to take care of the kids because you have another commitment, be sure you aren't leaving the children with an unsafe babysitter, since he might "yes" you but then not really be available for the kids. You might need to hire a sitter even if your husband might be in the house with the kids.

Now, let's say he's competent but just resistant or so busy that you have to work hard to tie him down to a commitment. Don't approach him with a demand or ultimatum like, "I've watched the kids all week and now it's my turn, so whether you like it or not, I'm out on Tuesday night starting at six, and you're going to have to deal with the kids or hire a babysitter."

If you need a night out or have a meeting to attend, approach your husband with a statement and a question: "I need to be out on Thursday night from six to nine, so we have to arrange for someone to watch the children. Will it work for you to be here, or do we need to find another alternative?" Give him plenty of notice if you have that luxury, and don't be apologetic; be calm and kind.

Most husbands don't have a clue where to line up babysitting help. True, if they had to, they might figure it out. (And keeping handy a list of potential babysitters is an excellent idea.) But do you really want to make this a fight between yourself and your husband? If your husband can't or won't be there when you need him, take responsibility for finding backup care.

But let's say that you have no available babysitters. Then you might make a stronger statement: "On Thursday night, I have to attend a meeting that is required of all managers at work. I'll need you to be available for watching the kids, because I haven't been able to find a babysitter. I'm giving you the heads up now. Is this going to be a conflict for you?"

Then the two of you need to discuss whose need will take priority and which one of you won't get what you want—this time. Conflicts happen frequently in a family with multiple demands on the parents.

Maybe your husband's attitude stinks: "You can skip that stupid meeting. What are they going to do—fire you? They need you too much. I'm not going to miss my bowling night just so you can chitchat with a bunch of your friends at work!" In that case, you've got a deeper problem in your marriage than finding a babysitter—your husband doesn't respect you or your work.

Claire, the mother of a young son, struggled with this issue:

> I learned to accept what I couldn't change and to work around it. My challenge came in my needing to attend evening social or professional activities and not having my husband home to baby-sit. It is virtually impossible to find a sitter for an hour between six and eight P.M. on weeknights. I solved this so now I schedule my daytime nanny to cover me when I want to go to evening events. It costs more, but it saves us from fighting that his job is too important and he can't or won't come home earlier.

Willingness to be involved with children and to share responsibility for their care is a huge part of permission to prosper.

Judy, a self-employed professional who occasionally has to travel for work, speaks for many working wives who are frustrated with the quality of child care that their husbands provide:

> I attended a conference for a couple of days, and my husband agreed to watch the kids: "No problem," he said. The day I was leaving, my nine-year-old daughter asked her father if he'd be home when she got out of school. He told her, "No, your sister (she's eleven) will be home with you." I asked him what was going on—he was supposed to take a couple of days off to be with them. He said he'd decided to go to work and that they were old enough to stay home by themselves. Then my daughter began throwing up—it seems she'd picked up the stomach flu. My husband just shrugged and went to work. I called in my cleaning lady, who spent the afternoon with my two kids, and the next day, my husband called my father to take over, instead of staying home with the kids himself.
>
> I was so mad at my husband I didn't talk to him for two days afterward. The inequity of it really rankled me, because even though he expects me to "bring in the bucks" when I'm working, I'm also expected to be home with the kids, do the shopping, clean out the fridge, wash dishes, and cook meals. But when I asked *him* to do that for only two days, he called in the backup and wouldn't even take off an hour to be with them.

There's little hope that Judy's husband is going to transform into Mr. Mom. She married him for better or worse, and this is one of the "worse" parts. The man is not a responsible father when it comes to watching the children, and it's not fair. He has a career, she has a career, so why should it all fall on her?

If your husband is not willing to be actively involved in parenting, refuses to spend time caring for the children, and insists that his work is always more important than yours, you have a choice to make. You can complain, whine, and nag, or you can focus on what you do love about him, appreciate the other ways he supports you and the children, and then pay someone to do his share of the job. Sometimes when a husband sees how much it's costing him financially, as well as in a lost relationship with his children, he'll wake up and rise to the occasion. And sometimes he won't, and you'll have to learn to live with the faults of the one you married.

Dealing with Burnout and a Short Temper

ONE OF the most common complaints working wives have is that their time with their children is limited, and then when they have it, they are too tired and short-tempered to make it quality time. Instead, their hours of parenting seem to consist of running the kids all over town for after-school sports and activities, supervising homework, making dinner and cleaning up, and disciplining the kids. After a long day at work, working wives crave the time to kick back and unwind before jumping into their Mom role, but they rarely get it. Downtime doesn't happen till late at night, when the kids are sleeping. No matter how energetic we are and how much we love our kids, this kind of daily grind wears down the best of us.

Many working wives end up shortening their workweek, because having children means medical appointments, sick children, children home from school for vacation, teacher conferences, snow days, school plays they don't want to miss, and the need to carpool to after-school sports and activities. Executive women feel the pressure of competing against professional men in the workplace who may have full-time wives taking care of all of these details. Working professional women feel squeezed between devoting the hours required to work and being there at essential moments for their children. If they are lucky, they share the burden with their husbands or they have help from a reliable nanny, but sometimes the kids just want Mom. One woman shared this:

> I cut my work day to a seven-and-a-half-hour day, and I also negotiated two unpaid days off per month to enhance the possibility of making doctor/dentist/emergency appointments with our children and to maintain my personal need for time alone.

Working wives must learn how to be there when it counts and to let go of regret when they can't be. Not long ago, I was preparing to attend a business conference. My seven-year-old daughter reminded me every day how sad she was that I couldn't be at the school play, in which she had a solo. Then she asked me if I wanted to hear her solo, and she sang it for me. I wished I could be there, and I told her that I knew it would be really special and I was very sad that I couldn't be there. I never suggested that it wasn't a big deal, because to her it was. I try to limit these conflicts by writing school events into my work calendar, but when I know I can't make it, I alert my husband, and one of us tries to be present.

If you find that you frequently miss moments with your children that are important to them, try prioritizing them as if they were important clients: write time with them into your calendar, and, as much as possible, schedule your work around their needs. If being flexible is impossible in your current career and time with your children is important to you, you may need to consider finding a different work situation.

Research has shown that except for special performances and holidays, the first ten minutes and last ten minutes of each day are the moments that your kids remember more than anything else. How you spend time with your children in the morning and before they go to sleep will be what sticks with them over the years. If you can't be there for the quantity of time you would like, you can make those twenty minutes as good as possible.

> No child will remember that the house looked a bit lived-in or that you bought them twelve Barbies instead of six, but they will recall the activities you did together. They want you to "be" with them, instead of acting annoyed because they are interfering with work you have to get done.
>
> —Robin

Dean shared with me his family's approach to ensure that both he and his wife got much-coveted quality time with their young daughter:

My wife and I have dedicated certain times of the day for each of us to be the lead parent. Because our daughter is home with me all day, I step back and let Mom take over shortly after she comes home, and she spends time with our daughter until her bedtime. While my wife and daughter are doing their thing, I make dinner. In the morning, we take turns getting her up and ready for school.

It may be helpful to designate a lead parent for certain times of the day and night so that each parent feels they get a real connection. The parents can swap on and off. The child feels cared for because one parent (or, in some families, a babysitter or nanny) is always there, and in any given moment it's clear who is in charge.

Working wives are often their own worst enemies, over-compensating for their absence at home by overdoing it outside of work. They enroll their children into more after-school activities than are good for the child (or manageable for the mother), and each night they work late into the evening to compensate for taking time off to be at every baseball game. They know they can't be there full-time for their kids, so when they can be there, they try too hard to be the perfect mothers.

> Women have this ability to multitask, and because we are capable of it, we abuse ourselves with it.
>
> —Meg Ryan, actor

I'll never forget the day I forgot to pack my seven-year-old daughter a school lunch. Her private school is a half-hour away, and it doesn't have a hot lunch program. I realized long after lunchtime was over that I had forgotten her lunch, and I'm glad I did, or I probably would have taken an hour out of my workday to drive her lunch to school. Instead, I worried throughout the afternoon about my poor, forlorn daughter with a working mommy who forgot to send her to school with lunch. I met her at the school bus with a big apology, and she only laughed and said, "Mommy, it was *so* cool—everyone shared their desserts with me, so I got to have a lunch with nothing but desserts. Would you please forget my lunch again?"

Every dual-career family has to decide who will watch elementary-age and preteen children when they are not in school—before school, after school, school holidays, school vacations, between end of school and when camp begins, sick days, snow days . . . Did I miss any? Oh, yes, when your child is having a rough time at school and needs a mental health day, too!

Often a woman and her husband will assume that the job for covering this time falls to her, unless she earns substantially more than he or is the family's clear breadwinner. This assumption can cause great resentment in the marriage.

I remember a year when my husband worked a straight job, I was self-employed, and we had the worst winter on record, with snow day after snow day for a period of weeks. Because I was self-employed, I watched the kids every day they closed school while my husband went to work. I had deadlines to meet, too, and the children were too young to occupy themselves while I worked, so it was a very stressful experience. My difficulties were nothing, though, compared with those of Ginny, a self-employed married woman who has a disabled child and a very difficult time balancing his needs with her career:

> When our baby son was chronically ill, I got very angry that my career took the brunt of all the caregiving. I went to the doctor over 100 times, almost all unscheduled. My husband's attitude was that I should be the one to do this, as he makes more money than me—which was his comeback whenever I complained that my career was being ruined and he didn't do enough to help during this two-year ordeal. I lost many clients and business due to this situation. It wasn't until my son's health improved that I

was able to put some time into my business and resurrect it. What hurt the marriage the most was the deep resentment I felt, and still feel, that my husband did not share the burden.

Did Ginny really need her husband to take care of the sick child half of the time? No, that's not what she needed. She was worried enough about the child; she naturally wanted to accompany him to the doctor for most of the visits or to be home with him when he was seriously ill. What she was missing was a feeling of respect from and true partnership with her husband. She wanted to be consulted. She wanted him to pitch in once in a while, to demonstrate that he agreed that her business, too, was important.

How do you get your needs met? First, you must figure out what they are. When your perception is so clouded with fairness issues and related demands, you might not truly know what you want or need.

To manage multiple demands on your time, you can use the same planning and organizational skills at home that you rely on at work. Map out the school calendar at the beginning of the year, or each month, and strategize with your husband how the time will be covered. Consider his time, your time, babysitters, after-school care, and other mothers in the same situation. The key to success is to expect numerous days when the children will be home throughout the year, rather than to be surprised by them. You can build a network of alternative child-care help, instead of attempting to somehow manage your career and child care at the same time.

If your fuse gets too short, reevaluate your career options and look for a better alternative. For me, that meant leaving corporate life in 1994 and becoming a work-at-home self-employed professional. I cannot conceive of managing all the demands of this house and our family if both my husband and I were locked into the rigidity of a corporate schedule. Other options: find a more accommodating supervisor, change fields, go from full- to part-time, take a leave of absence. It is a fluid process that changes as your children grow, as their needs change, and as your career evolves.

When you don't like the woman you have become and you no longer respect yourself, you can scarcely expect respect from your husband, your boss, or your children. Make a thoughtful choice, rather than act like a victim. "I quit my job because my husband wasn't supportive and I couldn't take the stress anymore" will get you sympathy from your women friends, but it will also make you feel bitter. Another way to view the situation is this: "My working full-time was too hard on our family, so I decided to prioritize our marriage and the children. I am looking for a different job that will work better for everyone."

It may be true that if you were married to the ideal husband, you could have kept the job. But if you plan to stay married to this guy, conceive of yourself as having made a positive decision for the sake of your marriage, rather than look at him as the enemy who took something precious away from you. If the resentment sticks with you, seek professional counseling as a couple to help you get past it.

Turning Resentment into Acceptance and Gratitude

DID YOU know you can change your attitude from resentment to acceptance and gratitude in a matter of seconds? It works about half the time for me. (The other half, I'm just too darn mad or too tired.) But half the time is pretty good.

Let's say you are feeling mama burnout and you're watching your husband as he sits on the couch, drinking a beer and playing with the remote. Perhaps you just want to throw something at him. Instead, say to yourself these simple words: "I get to."

When I'm exhausted and resentful about child-care burdens, I picture an infertile woman who has grieved all of her life over not being able to have children. When I'm fed up with trying to get my kids to go to bed, I take a deep breath, think of her, and say to myself, "I'm so lucky I get to do this."

When I look over my child's room that looks like a tornado came through and I feel myself getting steaming mad, I picture a woman who has a perfect nursery set up but no baby. That woman would love to have my mess to clean up.

When my children are all talking at once at the dinner table and the noise level is making me loony, I picture my husband and me as empty nesters, remembering fondly how the house used to be filled with children's laughter.

I know this sounds a lot like being grateful for the peas on your plate because there are people in Ethiopia who are starving, but this strategy works. Gratitude is the quickest antidote to resentment. No matter how frustrated you feel on any given day, you can always return to gratitude for the blessing of being a mother. No matter how annoyed you feel with your husband and your marriage on a bad day, it is still better than being alone. (Or so we hope!)

The Stay-at-Home Husband

YOU MAY be one of the rare women (fewer than 10 percent of all marriages) whose husbands take more responsibility for child care than do their wives. Some husbands not only "permit their wives to prosper"; they go a step further and give up their own careers so that their wives can focus serious attention on their careers. These rare circumstances usually occur when the wife is in the higher-paying field, when the husband is more suited by personality to take care of children, when the husband is in a job he doesn't like much anyway or can work from home, or when the husband is disabled or older and not as easily employable as his wife.

Friends of mine, Jennifer and Stephen, are undergoing a huge challenge. Jennifer relies on Stephen to take care of their four kids, ages seven, six, three, and one, while she works. Recently he fell off the roof and seriously injured himself, so Jennifer is juggling her full-time job, a husband in a wheelchair, and all of the children. She does so with humor, aware of how much worse it could have been and grateful that he is expected to make a full recovery.

Jennifer has always been open in her appreciation of Stephen, which has helped him adjust to the impact on his ego of having become "Mr. Mom":

> For a while, Stephen had it in his head that once the last child was in school, he'd go back to work. He realized not too long ago that the kids *are* his career, and he would not trade it for anything in the world. He has no plans to ever reenter the workforce, choosing instead his current occupation.

There are times when he questions what he's doing, but I—and friends, family, teachers, and strangers—often reinforce his esteem by telling him how well-behaved the children are and what a good job he's doing. One neighbor, whom we'd never met before, came all the way down to our end of the street, where Stephen was hauling a wheelbarrow full of rocks to his gardens. She introduced herself and said, "I see you outside with your kids all the time, and I just wanted to tell you that you are quite possibly the hardest-working man I've ever seen. I get tired watching you!" Boy, that sure made his day!

If you are lucky enough to have a full-time dad at home with the children, don't be surprised if "grateful" isn't the only emotion you feel. You may also feel jealous, envious, and resentful, wishing at times you could trade places with him. You could feel sad that you don't have more time with your children and think, "If I'd only married a man who could earn a better living, it could have been me, instead of him, home with the children!" It is natural to yearn for what you don't have and to think that your husband is the lucky one. (He's probably thinking the same thing about you on some days!)

Also, don't be surprised at how difficult it is at times to let go and allow your husband to move into what has always been defined as Mama's role. You are biologically and socially programmed to feel pangs of regret for not being your children's primary care provider. A certain amount of grieving is normal—just don't get stuck there.

Many families have a full-time parent for only a short period, then become a dual-career family once the children are of school age. Sometimes, too, mother and father will switch places depending on how the births of the children coincide with one parent's career options. Maybe the wife stays home when she is in law school, but when she joins a busy practice, the next baby gets Dad for a full-time parent.

Flexibility, open conversation, and lots and lots of expressed gratitude on both sides, regardless of who works and who stays at home, are the keys to making these arrangements work.

Together, you and your husband can find ways to share the joys and burdens of raising your children so that all of you prosper together. The key is to do it as a team, with an attitude of "We're in this together." When you stop demanding that your husband give equal time and start forgiving your husband for not punching the parenting clock the same number of hours you do, you open the opportunity for him to give you what you truly need, which is not just a clone of you.

CHAPTER SEVEN

Sex, Romance, and Stress

THE SEX life of most married couples ebbs and flows throughout the life of their relationship. A couple's sex life is a barometer of the intimacy of the couple, the time they have to spend together, their physical health, the number and ages of their children, the amount of money in their bank account, and many other outside stressors.

If you truly seek your husband's permission to prosper, the health of your sex life is worth some time and energy. A sexually satisfied man is a happier husband. (For that matter, a sexually satisfied woman is a happier wife.) How can you want sex more, create a satisfying sexual relationship with your husband, encourage him to give you what you need sexually, and all the while inspire him to support you emotionally in your career? Keep reading.

We wives would like to believe that a vibrant sexual life with our partners will naturally evolve from a close relationship; if we have to "force" it to be there, then something must be wrong with the relationship or with us. We fear that if we have sex when we're not in the mood, we are enslaving our bodies to our husbands' lusts, selling ourselves out like prostitutes. Cooking a nice meal to take away our husbands' grumpies, rather than granting them sex, may be more acceptable to our psyches.

The truth is, though, even the healthiest of relationships can go through cycles when one partner is less interested in or available for sex than the other. In a loving marriage, each partner learns to accommodate to the other's needs and to accept compromise. You can't possibly expect in a long marriage that every single week, year after year, both partners will crave sexual connection at exactly the same time, in the same manner. That's only the stuff of movies and romance novels. We can all relate to the following joke, which strikes a chord, as we chuckle about what it's like to fit sex on to our overburdened to-do lists.

Paul returns from a doctor's visit one day and tells his wife, Alma, that the doctor said he has only twenty-four hours to live. Wiping away her tears, he asks her to make love with him. Of course she agrees and they make passionate love.

Six hours later, Paul goes to her again, and says, "Honey, now I only have eighteen hours left to live. Maybe we could make love again?" Alma agrees, and again they make love.

Later, Paul is getting into bed when he realizes he now has only eight hours of life left. He touches Alma's shoulder and says, "Honey? Please? Just one more time before I die." She agrees, then afterward she rolls over and falls asleep.

Paul, however, hears the clock ticking in his head, and he tosses and turns until he's down to only four more hours. He taps his wife on the shoulder to wake her up. "Honey, I only have four hours left! Could we . . . ?"

His wife sits up abruptly, turns to him, and says, "Listen, Paul, I have to get up in the morning. You don't."

Sexual intimacy and satisfaction are closely tied to other factors in your marriage. You can please your husband (and be pleased yourself) without compromising your principles. And it is undoubtedly true that your husband will be more willing to encourage and support your career goals if he isn't feeling ignored and deprived physically.

According to Edward O. Laumann, Ph.D., coeditor of *Sex, Love, and Health in America,* half of Americans ages eighteen to fifty-nine have sex less often than once a week, and 30 percent of women each year report that they lack interest in sex for several months or more. You aren't "frigid" just because you and your husband aren't eagerly making love twice a week, the frequency most people believe is "normal" for a married couple. But if you are among the 30 percent of women who don't miss sex when it's absent, your husband is likely unhappy about living without sex for weeks and months at a time.

Did you catch the infamous scene in Woody Allen's movie *Annie Hall* where the lovers are talking separately to their therapist? He says they hardly ever have sex—"only three times a week." She says they have sex "all the time"— three times a week!

We've been brainwashed by the media with so many stereotypes about sex, it's hard for us to know what we really want. Do we truly want a husband who is so crazy about us that he lusts after us morning and night? We often want what we don't have—more sex if we aren't getting enough, and less if our husbands "bother us" for too much.

It's unreasonable to expect total satisfaction with your sexual relationship for every year of your marriage. Maybe the beginning years—BC (before children)—are your best, or maybe your best sex comes after you've been married for a number of years and have learned how to relax around each other. Perhaps your husband is in his sexual prime during the same decade that your libido is stuck in the mud. (It seems grossly unfair that a woman's sexual prime is in her forties, and a man's is in his twenties, doesn't it?) You are lucky if you and your husband coincide with your sexual desires for half of your marriage!

As with your waistline and your bank account, there will be fluctuating good years and others not-so-good, some great sexual moments, and a few evenings you're embarrassed to recall. The question isn't "How can my husband and I have a great sex life?"—as if there were some secret potion or pill that will magically transform a normal marriage into one continuous hot movie starring Julia Roberts and Mel Gibson. The real questions you should ask are: "How can I bring more mutually desired sex and romance into my married life, and how can I feel closer to my husband more days than not?" And in the context of the subject of this book, what does sex have to do with gaining the career support and cooperation from your husband that you crave? Ask a man who isn't getting any sex, and he'll tell you!

Diminished Sexual Drive and Its Consequences

MORE FREQUENTLY than not, the primary complaint from both men and women in a marriage that has moved out of its

honeymoon year is the decline of sexual interest and frequency over the length of the marriage. This issue is particularly relevant to dual-career couples with children and/or
demanding work schedules.

I've often thought that working wives would be far more interested in sex if they could multitask while doing it. For the
woman accustomed to finishing
two to five tasks at any one time,
it's a challenge to slow down and
allow herself the luxury of doing
only one thing—sexual connection with her husband—for maybe
as long as half an hour. (Inciden-
tally, the average length of sexual
intercourse between husband and
wife is eighteen minutes, start to
finish.) If she could make a phone
call, catch up on her reading, take
care of e-mail, and have sex at the
same time, she'd be a much more
available partner.

Unfortunately, sex often
winds up on a wife's list of things
to do. Since she can't do anything else at the same time, she
may delay sexual connection until she perceives she has the
time or inclination to totally chill out. It is no simple thing for
a busy career woman with a husband and children to move
herself out of "multitasking accomplishment mode" into re-
ceiver mode. If the woman is not able to make that mental
shift, unfortunately sex becomes another accomplishment on
her list—make him happy and give him what he needs—but

> Men who have sexual inter-
> course two or more times a
> week are 50 percent less
> likely to die from coronary
> heart disease than those
> who have sex less than once
> a month, according to re-
> search from the University
> of Bristol in England and
> Queen's University of
> Belfast. It sure beats the
> treadmill.
>
> —*Reader's Digest*,
> March 2002

without her becoming vulnerable and relaxed enough to receive affection and to enjoy sexual pleasure.

Even if she is a multitasker extraordinaire, it can be difficult for a woman to move between her different identities (soccer mom to account manager to sexy lover, for instance) all in the course of one evening. And health issues such as stress, illness, premenstrual syndrome, perimenopause, and sheer exhaustion can have a dampening effect on sexuality. (Oprah Winfrey caused quite a stir when she devoted a show to the topic of female disinterest in sex, with a guest doctor who recommended a testosterone cream guaranteed to significantly raise a woman's libido. Women rushed to their doctors by the thousands after the show aired. Alas, the issue is a bit more complex than any cream can handle.)

Despite the stereotype, it is not true that women always want less sex, while men always want more. Michele Weiner-Davis, author of *Divorce Busting*, states that low sex drive in men is vastly underreported. As many as 20 percent of husbands have a lower sexual drive than do their wives. This contradicts the popular notion that every husband is interested in sex with his wife any time he can get it.

However, since there's up to an 80 percent chance that your husband wants sex more often than you do, you do need to understand how sexual desire (or its absence) affects your marriage.

The man who thinks hundreds of times a week about sex with his wife may be slightly frustrated sexually, but it may actually be a good sign of the intimacy of their marriage. Set aside physical changes in one's body, the presence of children who demand time and energy, normal fatigue, and lack of

> W E CAN appreciate the male commitment to marriage more if we know that the average man under forty thinks of sex six times per hour, but the average married couple has sex 1.5 times a week. That means that a man thinks of sex over five hundred times for each time he has it.
>
> —Warren Farrell, Ph.D., *Why Men Are the Way They Are*

time, and you are still left with the largest reason for declining interest, the one you don't read about so much in current self-help literature: repeated criticism and dissatisfaction in the marriage.

Fatigue and exhaustion are physical states that can be transformed by a bit of affection, sexual energy, and caffeine. Resentment, criticism, and contempt, however, are seeping poisons that drain away any desire for sex.

Resentment and Lust
Are Incompatible Emotions

IF YOUR husband's self-esteem has been crushed because nothing he does is good enough for you (and that includes sex) or if he has emotionally shut down or hides out night after night in his home office to avoid fighting with you again, you could parade around in sexy underwear and leave a *Playboy* magazine on his night table with no effect. His sexual appetite has gone to sleep.

Maybe he's not in the mood much for sex anymore, because he no longer feels like Superman in your presence, and Clark Kent can't get himself sexually worked up when his Lois doesn't look at him anymore like she wants to be rescued or like he is her hero. A. Justin Sterling, author of *What Really Works with Men,* tells wives, "If you treat your man like a hero, you'll bring out the hero in him. He'll work hard to please you so he can keep being a hero in your eyes."

Criticism and resentment form a vicious circle. You feel no sexual desire because you're angry at your husband for letting you down again. He withdraws because your criticism shuts him down. Both of you feel hurt and misunderstood. If sex has dropped below cleaning out the gerbil's cage on the priority list or if every other word out of your mouth lately makes you sound like a nagging mother, it's no wonder that your sex life has dimmed. The satisfaction and frequency of your sexual relationship directly correlate with how well you are handling certain emotional hot spots in your relationship and how you prioritize your sexual relationship.

First, we'll take a look at six sources of male sexual dissatisfaction in marriage. (You can't fix what you don't understand.) Then we'll explore concepts you and your husband can work on together to improve both your sexual relationship and your likelihood of receiving permission to prosper. Again, your husband is less apt to view your work as competition when he knows that you have plenty of energy and affection for him. (In fact, you might want to share this chapter with your husband. Just think of the interesting conversations you can have—and who knows what might transpire in the bedroom afterward!)

Through His Eyes:
Why Sex Sometimes Isn't So Hot

1. "She's willing, but not eager."

Is bad or indifferent sex really so much better than no sex? If you ask a man who hasn't had sex in a long time, he'll probably nod. But ask a married man what it feels like to beg his own wife for sex, week after week, when she would clearly rather be washing her hair. He will tell you that it's hurtful.

Contrary to the stereotypes that abound about men and their perpetual horniness, sex is an emotional experience for a husband, too. If he gets sex with you, but no emotional connection, it's like getting cotton candy for dinner. It tastes good for a moment or two, but it leaves an empty, sick feeling in his stomach.

If your husband's urgent need for sex happens to coincide with a change in your work, it might not be testosterone that is driving his advances. Maybe his self-esteem is suffering, and he's looking for reassurance that you still find him attractive. Perhaps he's using sex to show himself, and you, that he's still in charge. Maybe he's really missing you, and the way he communicates that is through increased sexual desire for you. He could be angry at you, and sex is a form of domination for him. If you notice a change from the norm, talk to him about it and see if you can clarify the source of his increased passion. Maybe your newfound success, and any accompanying change in your aura, is a tremendous turn-on for him.

It's humiliating for a man to be controlled by his physical urges and to know that you are tolerating him only because you think of sex as your wifely duty, not because you really want to be sexually intimate with him. A man can experience sexual rejection as a tremendous blow to his ego. Some men, if they know their wives are merely accommodating them, will stop asking for sex even though they still crave it.

Your husband's feeling of rejection may be combined with resentment that he no longer comes first in your life but is usually third or fourth, after the job, the kids, and the house are taken care of. Why do so many Americans own dogs? We love the unconditional love and adoration we receive from them when we enter our home as they demonstrate their tremendous joy that we've returned after having been gone all day long. How do we greet our spouses now when we get home from work? Usually the dog makes out better.

Sex is an affirmation for him of his value as a man. In the absence of it, not only will he be physically edgy, but also he won't be anchored in the reassurance he gets that you love him when you share the intimate act of making love. Your husband may be reluctant to admit it, but it is important to him that he feel welcomed, appreciated, and adored at the beginning and end of the day.

Sometimes a husband creates the problem by assuming that his wife's active work life will dampen her availability for sex, thus setting up roadblocks for her prospering in a career, when in fact it could turn out to be just the opposite of what he fears. Many women, like Julia, find stimulating work to be, well, stimulating in other ways:

> When things are going well for me on a big project, I literally feel tingly all over. It must be the adrenaline that produces a creative high. When my mind and body are in that tingly phase,

not only do I lie awake thinking about the project, but also it makes me eager for sex. My husband is always delighted when a big project heats up, because he knows it doesn't just mean a nice check; it also means an active sex life!

When women like Julia are not creatively stimulated, they get crabby, drained, and distracted. Work is actually an aphrodisiac for these women, because when they are energized and feeling better about themselves, they feel sexy, assertive, and empowered—which translates to "hot" in the bedroom. Unfortunately, working wives like Julia are in the minority. For most working wives, more workload and a less-than-supportive husband translate into lowered libido.

2. "My wife and I fight so much, I don't even want to make love to her."

Women have long memories, and for many it may be months, even years, before they can forgive a major transgression in a marriage. But women may be more resilient than men when it comes to fighting. They are more able to express themselves in a fight and work toward some kind of resolution. They talk to their girlfriends, mothers, and coworkers, gather support, and get through emotional crises faster than their husbands. Often a husband's only close friend is his wife. Even if he has a few male friends he plays ball with or sees at church, he is unlikely to confide his marital troubles. So, when he and his wife are fighting, he's all alone.

Despite our recognized sensitivity, we women seem to be physiologically better prepared for the fallout of a heated fight. We don't run for the hills for quite so long as our lovers.

> I F YOU could just appreciate how difficult it is for men to express themselves in words, you wouldn't feel hurt and rejected when he doesn't say the things you want to hear. Men go through the motions of being sensitive, supportive, and nurturing, but invariably revert back to type when their backs are against the wall. You don't really succeed in feminizing your man, or if you do, you don't want him anymore.
>
> —A. Justin Sterling, *What Really Works with Men*

We may retreat because we are sulking, and we want to punish our husbands for doing something hurtful, but that's different from retreating out of fear.

For all their appearance of strength and machismo, many husbands are so sensitive to heated arguments or fights that they will do anything to avoid them, and once fighting starts in a marriage, they often retreat to protect themselves. A wife might reach out for more intimacy with her husband in the midst of a great deal of fighting; it's her way of trying to reconnect and to reassure herself that the union hasn't been destroyed.

During a marital battle, a wife may want reassurance that she isn't alone, whereas her husband may want only to be left alone. The difficulty some men have with multitasking applies to relating as well. A woman may be furious with her husband for something but still be able to relate to him—on a different channel, so to speak (unless she's chosen to give him the silent treatment). In an effort to resolve the fight, she may even talk more—a woman's usual method for resolving any kind of tension. Unfortunately, while the barrage of words that women fling at their husbands when they are angry looks like com-

I WENT TO talk to a counselor about my troubled relationship with my husband. He told me that at the time I least wanted to, in the height of an argument, I must go and put my arms around my husband and tell him I loved him. That moment occurred less than a week later. He and I were having an argument about something really silly, and I went over and gave him a hug and said that I loved him. It was one of the most difficult things I have ever done. It was also one of the greatest. He immediately melted into my arms, and we just hugged each other.

—Patty

munication, to the man on the receiving end, it feels more like a missile attack, so he dons his protective gear and takes cover.

The angrier or more scared a man feels, the likelier he is to withdraw. While a small percentage of couples have their best sex as "make-up sex" after a fight, most couples' sex lives suffer dramatically from frequently expressed anger in the relationship. Recurrent arguments and cold silences will damage every part of your relationship, including your sexual connection and any possibility that you will receive the permission to prosper you crave from your husband.

If you can't seem to refrain from damaging fights, seek professional help. Once disdain and screaming enter your relationship, you can do irreversible damage in a very short time. If professional help isn't in the cards, read a couple of classic books on the subject, like *Fighting for Your Marriage* or *We Can Work It Out*. Try to limit these emotional "discussions" to planned talks, perhaps with a marriage counselor,

> M Y HUSBAND and I are apart from each other all day long, with him home with the children and me working to support the family. So, we talk several times a day on the telephone. We make a point of never calling each other on the phone to complain—we reserve issues for face-to-face discussions. That way, we look forward to talking to each other!
>
> —Jennifer

rather than to blow steam at each other whenever the mood strikes you.

3. "She only wants to have sex when she's 'in the mood,' but if she would just give me a chance, I could help her get in the mood!"

What a vicious cycle—you haven't made love in so long, you don't even feel like a sexual being anymore. You're exhausted, and you're still mad at him because he forgot to pick up the kids this afternoon. Your mind tells you that you should have sex with your husband—after all, you're married to him—but it's as appealing to you as getting your teeth cleaned, something you know would be good for you but is hard to get excited about it. He makes overtures to try to get you interested, but you let him know right away: Not tonight.

Men do want more of an emotional connection during sex than women sometimes give them credit for. However, even when he's tired, your husband can usually get in the mood with a bit of foreplay from you. You are probably waiting for the emotional connection to appear first, which will then theoretically inspire you to want sex. But your husband often expects the sexual connection to come first, which releases his underlying emotional connection to you.

So, you and your husband may play a very unsatisfying game of "Who's going to make the first move?" Will you have sex when you aren't in the mood, hoping that it will put you in the mood, or will your husband agree to wait until you are feeling close enough to him to be an interested partner?

Many women enjoy sex once they are turned on, but it's getting out of the starting gate and overcoming inertia that is so difficult. If you enjoy sex once it's under way, but you are continually waiting until the perfect set of conditions inspires you to initiate it, experiment with inviting or allowing sex even when you aren't in the mood. Trust your body to remind you of why sex with your husband is a good idea. (This suggestion won't work if you genuinely hate sex; it's designed for the woman who likes sex once it's begun but has a hard time getting in the mood to start.)

Have you discovered that certain circumstances make it easier for you to make the transition from work mode to lover? To see what prods you in the direction of sexual interest, consider lighting special candles with an aroma you associate with sex or putting on a sexy lingerie or taking a shower before bed (even if you usually shower in the morning). You still might need to be convinced to go all the way, but your husband will be happy to help with that job if you'll open the door. You can even come up with a nonverbal signal. For instance, a certain candle may communicate, "I'm tired and not exactly feeling like a hot babe, but if you want to entice me into sex, I'm open to considering it."

4. "I'm just not turned on anymore by the way my wife looks."

Who ever said that your husband is supposed to be madly attracted to your body forever, when you aren't? We're not talking about the hypocritical guy who is a hundred pounds overweight and takes a shower twice a week and complains about his wife's having put on a few pounds. But I have empathy for the man who married a healthy, shapely woman, only to see her put on the pounds, stop exercising, and generally let herself decline over the years, turning from attractive lover to dragged-out career woman and mom before his eyes.

What really matters is *your* attitude toward your body. You may be a hundred pounds overweight, but if you love your body, spend the time to beautify yourself for your husband, and enjoy your sexual relationship, the weight may be no problem at all. In fact, some of the millions of women who fit the profile of the size six ideal hate their bodies! The real issue is not what you weigh. It's that if you feel so unattractive you deny yourself and your husband any sexual pleasure, because it's nearly impossible for a woman to enjoy sex when she is disgusted by her body and hides it from her husband.

Clothes may not "make the woman," but they don't hurt, either. Many women dress up beautifully for the office, but as soon as they get in the door, they can't get out of their "dress-up" clothes fast enough. Before they start cooking dinner, they kick off the heels and throw on the old *shmatte* ("rag") that they've been wearing since college. And that's what their husband sees when he comes home from work.

You certainly deserve to be comfortable and relaxed in your own home, but it may be worth your while to be attractive as well—especially if you want your husband's appreciation, cooperation, and support. Other husbands complain that their wives have become someone they don't recognize anymore. A woman may cut her hair short to look more "professional," dress up in power suits, and strip away some of the sexual aura that once turned her husband on. She may be stunning by corporate standards, but it's still an adjustment for her husband, who has to fall in love again with a new look.

Another issue is cropping up more and more in marriages with working wives. Call me old-fashioned (I wear the label proudly!), but it's also important not to dress in an overly provocative way when you go off to work. A husband is not being controlling when he requests that his wife keep her sexuality confined to their relationship. He may be proud of how gorgeous you are, but he doesn't want to worry about other men panting after you in the office. Besides, provocative clothing is not very appropriate for the office environment.

If you sense that something about your appearance is turning off or threatening your husband, invite him to tell you how your appearance at home (and in the office) is affecting his sexual interest in you.

You may believe you are entitled to dress and look any way you want. But if your husband is turned off by something about your appearance, there's nothing wrong with adjusting it to be more pleasing to him. If you do, make sure that you let him know that you are doing it just for him!

5. "My wife is a manager at work, and she doesn't know how to turn it off in the bedroom."

Some men need to lead when they're dancing, even if their wives are superb dancers. While your husband might fantasize about an aggressive woman in the bedroom, he also might prefer to connect from time to time with a softer, more vulnerable partner who allows him to be an initiator and to feel in charge.

When a woman spends her days in the office trying to turn off her charm so she won't seem inappropriate with employees, supervisors, and coworkers, it takes effort to shift gears and become a vulnerable, sexy wife. Female executives and business owners often adopt masculine energy in order to compete in the workplace; sometimes they take it home with them.

A working wife's assertiveness in the bedroom may be the welcome, positive outcome of her ability to love herself, her power, and her body. Many working wives report that their sex lives improve and they feel more attractive when they start feeling invigorated by life.

But, as always, you need to check in with your husband to see what turns him on. Maybe he's a bit intimidated by the "new you" and needs you to tame it a bit or to allow him to be the leader (at least part of the time) in your sexual interactions. The gift your husband can offer you, if you'll take it, is to create an oasis where you don't have to be "on," a place where you can be vulnerable and relaxed. I'll bet that even if you are quite superb at being the boss, you'd like to drop that role sometimes, to just be yourself and to receive, rather than always give.

6. "My wife tries hard to be loving, but she doesn't express her love the way I'd like it."

It's great that you keep a clean house, or that you make an awesome broccoli soufflé, or that you tell him all the time that

I WORK AT home, and so does my husband, so I'm around, but that doesn't mean I'm available. I tend to be very focused in my work, so sometimes it's difficult for me to stop what I'm doing and have a little conversation with my husband in the middle of the day, which is what he often wants to do. I'm learning to give that to him, though, because I look at it as an investment, like making deposits in a bank account. When I make a deposit in the love and affection account, it always comes back to me tenfold.

—Denise

you love him. If asked, he might say that you are a great wife. So what's missing? Maybe you are giving him love the way *you* want to receive it. A broccoli soufflé may not do it for him! Have you ever tried to think like him? How can you say "I love you" in a way he can really hear? Consider having sex that is out of the ordinary, throwing a Super Bowl party for him and the guys and getting out of the way, or putting the hottest jalapeño peppers you can find on homemade pizza for him. Saying "I love you" in your husband's particular language communicates that you are thinking just of him.

One day I ordered my husband a case of his favorite beer, for an outrageous price, from a distributor I found through the Internet. He had mentioned casually to me that he hadn't had this beer since he'd discovered it in Germany while traveling there as a college student. It took half an hour of my time to do the Internet search and about a hundred dollars to order the beer because of the shipping cost. Yes, part of me was thinking, "What a big waste of money—we could have purchased a new mixer for the kitchen!" But this was a present strictly for him, and he thoroughly enjoyed it.

You might be surprised to discover what really makes a difference to your husband. It could be something he wishes you would do, or not do, and he might not tell you about it. You'll have to be a detective and discover it by his behavior or his casual remarks.

Vicki discovered that her well-intentioned desire to work extra hours in her business to ensure its success was unintentionally separating her from her husband in a way that was bumming him out:

> When I first started my business, I was staying up late, working, and getting to bed around three in the morning. My husband has to get up early for his own job, and he started to sleep in the spare room so that he wouldn't get disturbed by me coming to bed. We did this for only a week, and then I realized that sleeping in separate beds was really hurting our relationship. I started going to bed at the same time as my husband and getting up earlier with him to put in the extra working hours.

Some couples highly value going to sleep at the same time, and others don't. Maybe another husband would have a different preference—for example, that he be encouraged to sleep separately for a better night's sleep but that they plan a "sex date" once a week rather than wait for it to occur spontaneously. There are no rights or wrongs here, only what works for the two of you. When in doubt, ask your husband, and pay attention to the clues that he gives you. They are plentiful if you are looking for them.

Through Her Eyes: Why Sex Sometimes Isn't So Hot, and How a Better Sex Life Can Translate into More Prosperity

HOW-TO BOOKS on marriage and sex abound; walk into any bookstore and you'll find dozens of them. But you're reading this book because you want to learn how to encourage your husband to give you permission to prosper. And what does your own sexual satisfaction have to do with that? The more satisfied you are in the bedroom, the more inspired and motivated you'll be to care for your husband in the ways that encourage him to be more loving toward and supportive of you. And a woman thrives on an intimate sexual connection with her husband, which in turn can fuel the energy she relies upon to build her career. A win-win, positive spiral.

> More than beautiful women, it is the sweet, kind, smiling ones who hold a man. Get into the habit of greeting your husband with a warm, loving smile, because that's what makes a man feel, "This is my home, this is where I belong."
>
> —Rebettzin Jungreis,
> *The Committed Life*

1. *Keep criticism out of the bedroom, and limit it in the other rooms as well.* If your self-esteem soars at work and you're feeling enthusiastically cheered on by your husband, life is likely to feel easier. But if you're ridiculed constantly at home and attacked for every fault and flaw, life outside your marriage can begin to look pretty appealing. Just as a husband needs to feel good about his relationship with his wife, and also about himself, so a wife needs

to feel accepted and loved unconditionally—especially if great sex is on the agenda.

Why is your husband criticizing you or complaining at every opportunity? He may have an idea of the perfect wife, and your attachment to your career is not part of that picture. He has to learn how to fall in love with the real, emerging you, rather than with his fantasy of the perfect wife. Only a mature, loving, self-confident man can applaud as his wife comes into greatness. You may need to help your husband become one of those men by soothing his fears and meeting his needs that, when unmet, result in anger and criticism.

Don't just start working longer hours at work to avoid your critical husband. Tell him that you are starting to dread coming home because of his constant complaining, and he needs to get a grip. If you have always tolerated your husband's being critical of you and you haven't truthfully revealed to him how much it hurts, he may not "get it" until you threaten to end the marriage or have an affair. I hope you can find a way to deliver the message to him before it goes that far.

If your husband asks for sex after a particularly difficult day and it's not at all appealing to you, tell him clearly, "I'm not interested," but don't do so by insulting him or by turning away physically and giving him the cold shoulder. Instead, say something like, "The way you spoke to me about (blank) really hurt, and it killed my desire for sex. I'd love to want sex with you, but I'll need your help getting warmed up to you again." Your husband might not understand how the words or tone of voice he uses, or his lack of praise for your dinners, correlates to your waning libido. Once he gets the message, you might be criticized less and adored more.

2. *You can't ignore a partner and expect much of anything in re-*
turn—including sex. Perhaps you've heard this joke: "My wife
claims I never pay any attention to her. At least I think that's
what she said." Women and men have probably been fighting
over this issue since Adam and Eve. He complains that he's
not getting enough sex, and in the few moments they have together right before sleep or upon waking, he asks, begs, or
hints for it. After she's worked the second shift—spending
hours after work taking care of kids and house with scarcely
any help from her husband—and knowing she has to get up
early in the morning for her job, the last thing on her mind is
sex. If he would try offering to put the kids to bed, he could
see how fast she perks up.

Rabbi Shumuley Boteach, coauthor with Uri Geller of
The Psychic and the Rabbi, shares this insight:

> The leading complaint I hear from wives about their marriages
> is that their husbands ignore them. Instead of talking, they
> watch television or play on their laptops. Can you imagine that
> someone finds their life so stultifyingly boring that rather than
> speak to his wife, he would rather someone else speak to his
> wife? And rather than watch his own wife undress, he would
> rather watch someone else's girlfriend undress? We are no
> longer escaping life into fantasy with *The Wizard of Oz* and
> *Star Wars.* We're escaping life into someone else's life. I recently
> saw a late-night celebrity interview with one of America's lead-
> ing movie actors. For twenty minutes he told the most banal
> story of how he had burnt lasagna in his kitchen and his con-
> certed efforts to remove the black melted cheese from the bot-
> tom of the pot. Any wife who would have spent twenty minutes

to tell her husband a similar story would have sent him into a deep coma.

A wife ignored at home is at a higher risk for a marital affair in the office. Some men have legitimate reasons to worry that their previously loyal wives will be tempted into an affair. If a woman is not nurtured, cherished, or given affection at home—and starts getting those needs met at the office by a successful, appreciative, attentive colleague or boss—the temptation can become quite strong, no matter how strong her moral fiber and commitment to fidelity.

John Gray, Ph.D., author of *Men Are from Mars, Women Are from Venus,* has an excellent approach to this problem. He asks men to think about how they treat their clients. Then he points out that their wives aren't getting the same first-class treatment. (This applies to many working wives and *their* husbands, too). Dr. Gray followed his own advice with good results:

> Instead of seeing eight clients a day, I started seeing seven. I pretended that my wife was my eighth client. Every night I came home an hour earlier. I pretended that my wife was my most important client. I started giving her that same devoted and undivided attention I would give a client. When I arrived home, I started doing little things for her. The success of this plan was immediate. Not only was she happier, but I was too.

3. *Be sure to make time for sex and romance.* I know from experience how scarce romantic time is in a dual-career household, especially if you have children. It helps to set aside at least half an hour each day for romance; if that's impossible, try for half

an hour each week. You can't find half an hour a week for romance? I don't buy it. You may not think half an hour will accomplish anything, but it can transform your marriage.

According to William J. Doherty, Ph.D., married couples spend on average only thirty minutes a day together. You might be in the same house for longer than that, but you are probably together only half an hour, if you don't count sleep time. So, will you use your precious time together well? I'm not going to lecture you about the need for more time (although that helps). Instead, let's look at how to better use the few minutes you've got.

Here's where rituals make a huge difference. Every couple's got them, and rituals are very different from routines that hold no emotional significance. Maybe you always kiss goodbye before going to work, even if you are mad at each other. You hug good night. You watch the evening news together before bed. You speak at lunchtime for five minutes. You e-mail a few times a day. Each of these connections takes only a few minutes. But busy dual-career couples often make a lethal mistake: They drop important rituals that take only a few moments, because they get "too busy."

Rituals are the glue that holds a family and couple together. Connecting at the beginning and end of the day is particularly powerful. If two careers make it impossible for *all* of your previous rituals to continue ("We never used to miss a meal together, but now we often eat apart"), don't let it go below ten minutes minimum, every day. At the very least!

A few suggestions: Give each other a five-minute neck rub. Ask your spouse how his day was at work, and listen when he answers. Call or e-mail once a day just to say, "I love you," and keep logistics out of that communication. Look for

A S I was sitting at my computer, my husband came in with a bowl of udon for my lunch. He set it down beside me, then quietly left the room. It was a small gesture, but through him, I am slowly learning that I can have connection without submission, domesticity without a betrayal of self. Those lessons did not come easily to a woman whose feminism was built on the primacy of autonomy and achievement, who saw any step toward traditional spheres of femininity as backsliding.

—Peggy Orenstein, *Flux*

one small act of kindness to do for each other every day— something that lets your spouse know that you are thinking of him. Pray together.

Kiss your husband on the lips before he leaves for the office, and tell him you think he's sexy. If your spouse is reading a book, ask him what it's about, and really listen to his answer. Put a favorite CD of your mate's on the stereo, even if it's Neil Diamond and you prefer hard rock. Bring your spouse lunch.

If you can't organize your life together so that you have ten minutes of kid-free, uninterrupted time a day, you may be falling into a common working-wife trap: You are giving all of your time to your children to compensate for working. No child is going to benefit from divorced parents. You are taking good care of your kids when you keep your marriage strong, and beyond that, you are teaching your children how to create healthy adult relationships in their future marriages. When you put your marriage last, you only hurt your kids, now and in their adult lives.

When you and your spouse have a precious five or ten minutes together, or even a whole evening, don't spend your time complaining. Enjoy the moment. Someday you'll be retired and the children will be grown, and you'll have lots of time together. You'll enjoy those years only if you've kept the intimacy alive when you were younger.

4. *Sexual and physical energy comes from healthy bodies.* I know how hard it is to squeeze it all in. Physical fitness is often one of the first activities, other than sex, to drop away. Busy working men feel entitled to devote leisure time to a hobby or sport, even if it deprives their wives and children of time as a family or a couple. Women perpetually feel guilty if they do something that seems selfish, like physical fitness. But of course, it's not selfish at all.

When you pamper yourself and keep your body in shape, you work more effectively, you are nicer to your family, and you are more interested in sex.

If it's a time management issue, find a sport or form of exercise that allows you to multitask. I read and pray on the treadmill, and I write (in my head) or pray while I'm swimming laps at the gym. What can you do without losing efficiency? If you make it simple and keep it regular, a few hours a week will make a big difference in your fitness level.

As you become more successful in your career, beware of an increase in addictive behaviors, such as overeating, drinking, and workaholism. These are tempting habits to fall into, especially when they are well-intentioned efforts to deal with your stress. Get real with yourself—you know that when you feel lousy in your body, everything else is more difficult. If cooking healthy meals is too taxing after a full day's work, invest in hiring a personal chef at least a few times a week—your body is worth it!

Men have learned how to put themselves first, and this is one place where women need to take a lesson from their book. If you can't stand the idea that you are making yourself more important than your husband and children, tell yourself it's all for them anyway. Maybe you are married to a guy who says he wants to see you take better care of yourself, but it's just lip service: he blocks you from taking the time you need. In that case, establish certain bottom-line commitments, and don't let yourself get pulled out of them every week.

Be realistic. If your husband objects to your running a few miles a week, don't just announce to him one day that you are going to start running ten miles a day whether he likes it or not and he can do his own damn laundry from now on because you won't have the time anymore. How supportive will he be? Enroll him in your dream, and invite him to suggest how the two of you can make it happen. Give him warning about what he'll have to pick up the slack on in order for you to have the time you need. Set a realistic goal to work up to. If you aren't doing any exercise at all, finding an hour three times a week would be a major accomplishment. Once your husband and the kids know that you are serious about taking better care of yourself, they will respect your commitment more, and they might even be inspired to take better care of themselves.

5. *Beware of the sex-killing effects of exhaustion.* We'll devote chapter 8 to tensions in your marriage regarding household chores. The strategies you'll read there are bound to dramat-

> I'M A professional sewer, and my husband is an assembly line worker who doesn't know anything about sewing. But the other day we watched a sewing show on PBS that fascinated me, and my husband watched it with me, just because he knew that I found it interesting. What a sweetie he is!
>
> —Cheryl

ically improve your sex life. For now, here are some quick thoughts on the relationship between fatigue and sex.

Your husband may need your help in understanding the correlation between how much sex he gets and how much help you get. If he's an intuitive guy and he wants more sex, he'll start "loving you" more the way you want to be loved. He may be clueless or lazy or feel that his doing housework is demeaning, but don't measure his love for you by the yardstick of housework done, or you'll be resentful for no reason.

The most important lesson husbands need to learn is that sex begins for most women outside of the bedroom. You can have foreplay with your clothes on, across the room from each other, once he starts picking up the kids' toys, cleaning the kitchen, giving you helpful advice for your business, and generally acting kind, supportive, and eager to help.

What you also need to understand is that the same goes for your husband, even though we don't often speak in the same way about men and foreplay. As we've noted before, you can turn him on or off according to how you speak to him outside of the bedroom. Will you be his "mother" or his lover? When both you and your husband start expanding your thoughts about sex and romance beyond physical pleasure and what takes place in your bed to how each of you treats the other throughout the day with your thoughts, actions, and speech, both of you will likely enjoy a more rewarding sexual relationship.

If fatigue is your number one turnoff for sex with your husband, be straight with him. Give him a dozen ideas for how he can relieve your workload, and let him know that he'll be happy with the results if he starts being more of a partner in the home. You don't have to do it tit for tat ("You sweep, we have sex"), but you can let him know—not just in words but in your actions—that when he's more helpful with the kids and the house, you feel more amorous than usual.

Now, let's examine how you can fix your household burden and fire up your sex life at the same time. Nothing like clean dishes and a night off from cooking to coax those embers into flames.

CHAPTER EIGHT

Household Responsibilities and Stress

I ONCE INTERVIEWED a woman who had become a real estate agent late in her marriage, after her children were in high school. For twenty-five years, she had washed and ironed her husband's shirts for him. After a particularly grueling weekend of work, her husband came to her on Sunday night and said, "Honey, I have no clean shirt to wear to the office tomorrow." The woman went ballistic. She turned his laundry basket upside-down and shouted, "Do it your-f . . . ing-self!"

This situation wasn't her husband's fault; she had always done his shirts for him. She assumed that he would see how tired she was and suddenly feel compelled, out of compassion for her and a sense of teamwork, to do the shirts himself. Such assumptions can be the kiss of death in a marriage. New agreements must be reached each time a marriage goes through a change or transition. In cases like these, women sometimes throw up their hands in righteous indignation, but their husbands are only doing what they have always done. It's the woman's responsibility to communicate changing needs to her husband, rather than to assume that he'll instantly transform himself into the ideal partner and helpmate.

I hope by now you are so imbued with teachings from the permission-to-prosper philosophy that the subject of household duties will be easier to deal with. There is no topic that makes working wives more irate than the gross unfairness of carrying the lion's share of household responsibilities despite their working as hard as, or harder than, their husbands outside of the home.

Many women accept that even after they begin work, they will continue to bear the primary responsibility for parenting, that younger children in particular need the nurturing that only a mother can provide. (Although some fine stay-at-home dads would take issue with this assertion.) But the same argument doesn't fly where housework is concerned. Most women don't see why it requires a female to vacuum the carpet or wash the laundry. If their husbands are intelligent enough to manage a multimillion-dollar budget, certainly they can figure out how to turn on the dishwasher.

Not too long ago, men and women made an implicit agreement upon marriage: In exchange for receiving his financial support, she took care of him, which included doing the laundry and ironing, cooking meals, straightening the house, running household errands, and caring for the children. Her end of the bargain was clear. Even if she hated cleaning or wasn't a very good cook, she was expected to give it her best, with a smile.

Now the assumption that a woman will clean and a man will work is null and void, eradicated by women's entrée into the workplace. So, how do we explain and make peace with the

STUDIES SHOW that 80 percent of the conflicts raised by the wife are about household issues. Frequently, that puts the husband in an awkward position. While not concerned about the problem, he is asked to help resolve it. If the married man recognizes the validity of his wife's concerns, then constructive work can begin on the problem.

—Scott Haltzman, M.D., psychiatrist

latest research, which demonstrates that a woman's responsibilities in the home scarcely lessen after she returns to work?

Susan Maushart dedicated an entire book to this inequity. In *Wifework,* she reports:

> Research conducted throughout the English-speaking world continues to show that wives, whether employed or unemployed, perform 70 to 80 percent of the unpaid labor within families. Husbands whose wives work full-time for pay do no more domestic labor than husbands of women who are not in paid employment at all. Wives also contribute 100 percent of the husband care—the myriad tasks of physical and emotional nurture that I call "wifework." Wifework is a time-consuming, energy-draining, and emotionally exorbitant enterprise. Centered primarily on the care and maintenance of men's bodies, minds, and egos, wifework is a job that violates every principle of equal-opportunity employment—often, chillingly, in the name of love. There is no counterpart to wifework, no reciprocal husbandwork driving males to provide caregiving to their female partners at the expense of their own well-being.

Arlie Russell Hochschild, the author who coined the expression that's also the title of her book, *The Second Shift,* draws basically the same conclusion: "Because of the second shift (household responsibilities women take on after they complete their first shift of paid work outside the home), women work fifteen hours longer each week than men. Over a year, they work an extra month of twenty-four-hour days."

No wonder so many women are angry and tired. The following joke is a social commentary on how women feel about household responsibilities while working:

A woman is sitting at a bar, enjoying an after-work cocktail with her girlfriends, when an exceptionally tall, extremely sexy young man enters. He is so striking that the woman cannot take her eyes off him.

The young man notices her overly attentive stare and walks directly toward her. Before she can offer her apologies for so rudely staring, he leans over and whispers to her, "I'll do anything, absolutely anything, you want me to do, no matter how kinky, for $20—with one condition."

Flabbergasted, the woman asks what the condition is.

The young man replies, "You have to tell me what you want me to do in just three words."

The woman considers his proposition for a moment, then slowly removes from her purse a $20 bill, which she presses into the young man's hand along with her address. She looks deeply, longingly into his eyes, and slowly, meaningfully says, "Clean my house."

Many husbands agree in principle that it's only fair for them to help more in the house, but too often it is lip service only. Husbands may "help," but they don't own responsibility for the household the way that wives do. A husband who refuses to share the burden of household work isn't giving you permission to prosper; you cannot throw your full energy into your work when you were up until midnight the night before, cleaning the bathroom, and even if you are getting enough sleep, tensions in your marriage brewing from your resentment have a way of deflating and distracting your energy. Permission to prosper means, by definition, that a husband helps his wife thrive in her career. Many women need a true team player at home for that to happen.

We wives have traditionally responded to the housework dilemma in one of four ways:

1. We go on strike, refusing to do more than half of what is needed at home. If our husbands don't do their fair share, it doesn't get done. Our homes aren't as clean as our mothers', and our dinners are fast-food more often than we'd like, but that's the price we pay for a dual-career household.

2. We hire people to do what our husbands don't do and what we can't get to anymore. We hire personal chefs, housekeepers, gardeners, dog walkers, and errand services. I'm sure that if we could hire someone to exercise for us, we'd do that, too.

3. We bitch and complain about our lazy husbands and do most of the work ourselves. We give up trying to change him—or we knew from the beginning that nagging would be useless. Over time we learn to stop feeling resentful—at least we hope so—and start accepting his faults as something we've just got to live with.

Faith Hill, the Grammy award–winning singer, is a good example of a woman who has learned to laugh at the man she knows is never going to share her responsibilities at home. (It's easier to laugh when you are wealthy enough to pay someone to pick up the slack!) She shared this in a magazine interview:

> My husband, Tim, and I are pretty much half-and-half, especially when it comes to the kids. The only thing he doesn't do is clean. Over the Christmas holidays, he cleaned more than I have seen him clean, ever. I mean, he was picking things up! I was so impressed. Then one night we're lying in bed and he turns to me and says, "Okay, I'm done. No more cleaning." It was like, Okay, I've filled my quota for the year.

4. We do all of the above, as well as work on influencing our husbands to be our partners at home, without having to constantly beg for it. That is the approach we'll concentrate on in this chapter. It helps a lot, though, to also lower your standards a bit. You can find a balance, the middle ground between a perfect home and one that is a pigsty. You may choose to hire help whenever it is feasible, or do more than half the work, but you can follow through with an open heart and peace in the home, instead of anger.

Unless your husband is one of the rare ones, or a stay-at-home dad, he's probably not ever going to do half of the household work, so stop asserting that he ought to and fuming when he doesn't live up to your expectations. But if you can convince your husband to help you more than he currently does, take heart.

Household responsibilities are not just a woman's issue. Our husbands suffer, too, when we are angry, tired, nagging wives who don't want sex as often as our husbands would like. Your husband may be more eager to resolve this problem than you think; settling the housework issue once and for all will relieve a great deal of stress in the marriage.

On one level, we all need to lighten up a bit and adopt more of Arlie Russell Hochschild's attitude: "Why wreck a marriage over a dirty frying pan? Is it really worth it?" And yet, if in your home you can't resolve who is going to clean the frying pan, you probably aren't creating a home of peace, love, and respect, either.

Sometimes hopelessness sets in because you can't break free of the same old argument that spins around and goes nowhere, which starts something like this: "You should help me more. I work, too!" Maybe you find that the repeated fights about "who does what, when, and how" feel like the quip Michele Weiner-Davis, author of *Divorce Busting,* made once: "I jokingly say that instead of doing the same old argument over and over, couples should just say to each other, 'Honey, we haven't done argument number seven for a long time, so why don't we do it tonight?'"

Why a Husband Often Refuses or "Forgets" to Help Around the House

AS WE near the end of this book, we have come to understand that a husband's rationalization and defense are often a disguise for deeper conflicts brewing. He knows he can't get away with complaining that he is tired from work (because his wife is, too), that he wasn't raised doing housework (because he is smart enough to learn), or that he doesn't notice what needs doing (because his wife is happy to tell him). Wives don't take their husbands off the hook after hearing those excuses—so, often, their husbands vow to do better but with mixed results.

Does your husband "forget" to pick up the eggs on the way home as promised or procrastinate doing what he agreed to do until you, in exasperation, just do it yourself because it seems easier than nagging him (which is, of course, what he is hoping for at least some of the time)? Join the club you'd rather not belong to!

If this were really an issue of your husband not having enough time because of his busy career, you would expect that the more time he spent at home, the more housework he'd do. Especially in female breadwinner households with stay-at-home dads, you'd envision men who have learned how to play the role of Mr. Mom, right?

Surprisingly, even though a man might agree to take care of the kids during the day, only a small number of men show promise in the cleaning and cooking categories. Even full-time stay-at-home dads still leave most household cooking and cleaning to their wives or hired help, even if they are home all day.

So, what is this household responsibilities issue really all about? It has to be more than an allergy to dusting.

Who Does What, When, and How: It's All About Power

OUR QUEST for equal power in our relationships with our husbands has come crashing into the old-fashioned and politically unpopular notion that housework and cooking are "women's work." One reason working wives often run into stubborn or self-centered husbands who refuse to do their fair share is that while men may not believe they have the right to demand being waited on by their working wives, *they still want it.*

Most men know they should be helping more, but they don't want to—or genuinely can't—figure out a way to do so, because they can't juggle multiple and conflicting priorities as masterfully as women. It may also be true that men are "tired" in a different way than their working wives are.

Working wives work as hard as—and sometimes harder than—their husbands do, but only one-third of women are the primary earners in their families. A man may drain his energy more at work because of the pressure he feels to succeed and to provide for his family. Millions of women want to succeed; still, fewer of them have to worry as much as men do about the financial consequences of failure.

So, when a man comes home from work, he could be genuinely more wiped out than his wife is. Also, if there are children in the home, a man may not be able to juggle kids and household chores at the same time, so he often prioritizes the kids.

A man is socialized from his earliest years to spend his time either pursuing work that will earn him accolades, status, and money or, in modern times, spending more time with his kids so he can be an involved father. A wife can "should" her husband into picking up more housework at home, but he doesn't gain status or recognition from peers by succeeding in this arena. Your husband may not win accolades from you either, especially if your attitude is, "Why should I thank him for doing his fair share? He lives here, too. I'm not his maid!"

Today, unfortunately, a woman often feels shame if she is a full-time housewife—she needs to add, "Because I take care

THERE APPEARS to be a huge difference between the definitions of "support" between men and women. I've talked with many women, and when they say their spouse is supportive, often what they mean is that their spouse isn't actively sabotaging their career or professional efforts. When a woman is supportive, she has dinner on the table and the kids are taken care of and she's running the books and doing the administrative work for her husband's business as a third job.

—Denise

of our children full-time." Caring for children earns some recognition (although not enough), but if she's spending her time taking care of the home and her husband, others may convey a lack of respect or appreciation for her commitment. Isn't there more a woman should be doing with her time than cleaning and cooking?

If a woman doesn't feel valued by our society for the work she does at home, then why should a man value the work his wife does at home or consider it a good use of his time to share in the responsibilities? Having been socialized to pursue recognized status symbols (the big salary, the new Mercedes, the beautiful wife, the kids in private school), men will not instinctively be drawn to achieving in the realm of household responsibilities. There is, as women well know, no power and little recognition in a spotless floor.

Besides his reluctance to do what he considers demeaning, unrewarding work—and his skill deficits because he didn't have any role models to learn from—there's another significant reason why your husband isn't helping more at home: You might keep taking over and doing it yourself, usually because he doesn't do it "right" or on time. Most men are not stupid. They figure out quickly that if they are willing to tolerate a bit of friction and nagging, they can escape the job—maybe forever!

How to Avoid "Managing" Your Husband— and How to Manage Him Successfully When It's Necessary

THIS SUBJECT certainly hits home for me. I am increasingly aware of how often I want to boss my husband around like an employee. I want him to help with more household responsibilities, and I get angry at and tired of the occasional inequities in the house. But even if Stephen agreed to do half of the work, I would still want to direct what he does, when, and how. Essentially, I, like many women, want to be supervisor of the household, with my husband as my servant.

I may say I want a true partner, because that sounds good, but that would mean giving up some control. Truthfully, I want my husband to do half of the work—but I want to tell him what to do and how to do it. I want to pull out my "honey-do" list every day and, as soon as he wakes up or finishes work, be entitled to say, "Listen, dear, this is what I need you to do!"

That kind of approach is not okay with Stephen, or with most men.

The single most important reason men do less work around the house than do women is that most men refuse to give up autonomy over deciding what they are going to do and when. Most men follow instructions all day long at work. The last thing your husband wants to do is give up his precious autonomy at home, too. If he is willing to help, he wants to be able to choose what tasks he'll do, and he insists on control over his schedule.

I've had to learn over the years to live with this requirement from my husband. If I need something done urgently, I'll tell him. But if I just *want* something done now and it's not urgent, I have to back off, ask for his help, and then wait patiently for him to get around to it, according to his own schedule. This conflict has created great tension at times in our household, as my idea of when I need something doesn't always jibe with my husband's!

This dynamic leads, of course, to the tendency to do it myself if I am capable, when he isn't willing to respond to my time schedule, or when he doesn't do it my way. Women incessantly complain, "Why should I ask him to clean the bathroom, since I have to do it over again myself when he's done?" Or "If I leave him in charge of the laundry, he waits until every last piece of clothing is in the hamper, and then I have to worry about whether the kids will have clean clothes to wear for school."

In many homes across the nation, tired, frustrated women resort to "doing it myself"—which of course only makes the problem worse. The upper class deal with this frustration by hiring "wives," but many lower- and middle-class families cannot afford to hire help—sometimes they *are* the help! In those situations, it isn't going to get done unless Mom, Dad, or the kids do it.

Husbands will not leap to do housework if we approach them like supervisors, ordering them around. This has nothing to do with what's fair. It's about what works, or doesn't work, when it comes to the males we married. The guy just isn't going to do it if you order him to.

Research shows that women do most of the household work that requires a daily commitment (and there's little flexibility over when the job is done), while men do more of the household jobs that show up from time to time (gardening, auto maintenance, fixing the toilet). Even if a man agrees to take on a regular job in the house, he will do it his way, and if you don't like his way, you'll have to shut up or be willing to do the job yourself. Just as men are willing to do certain tasks that are comfortable or convenient but not others, we wives would like to keep certain responsibilities—because that way it's done right—but give away the tasks that drain us or the ones where we don't care so much about results. When it comes to our chores, if we can't hire it and our husbands won't do it, and we consider it essential, we do it.

You can teach even the most seemingly inept husband how to do that which needs doing in the home. You can say, "Here's how you turn on the washing machine, and please don't put David's church pants into the dryer, because they'll shrink." But you might not always get your version of doing the job right. See if this conversation sounds familiar: You say, "I told you to fold his pants on the crease so that they won't need ironing. Now one of us needs to iron his pants before church!" To which your husband responds, "Give me a break. They don't need ironing—he's only eight years old!" So you reply, "I don't care if he's five or twenty. He's not going to church looking like he just rolled out of bed. If you can't make sure that his pants are presentable, I'll just have to do his wash myself." And he responds, "Sure, go ahead!" And there you are, doing the wash yourself—again.

You may have to work at closing the gap between your husband's request to do a job on his schedule and your desire to have it done within a certain time frame. One solution is to give your husband a range of time to work with: "I'd appreciate it if you could do this sometime in the next three days" rather than "Can you do this right now?" or "Please take care of this." (Too vague—one week later, you'll still be waiting, because it didn't make his priority list and you weren't clear about when you wanted it done.)

The goal is that your husband will learn not to "yes" you and then "forget" to do it. Instead, he will say something like, "I agree that needs to be done. If I don't get to it this weekend, I'll do it sometime during the week. How does that work for you?" Then hope that he will follow through and do as promised. The key is to work these requests out as a cooperative team. This process will undoubtedly take time and practice to become habit.

Here's another tip I've learned over the past decade: Sometimes, if it's really important to you that a job be done a certain way, you do need to do it yourself, but you don't have to get mad at him for it. For example, my husband is perfectly willing to clean the dinner dishes but on his schedule, which means they could sit in the sink overnight and still be looking at me at breakfast time. That's not okay with me—having dirty dinner dishes in the sink at breakfast is revolting to me.

So, Stephen doesn't wash dishes after dinner. Now, I could get mad at him (and I used to), but in fairness to him, it's my issue, not his, that I want the dishes washed right after dinner. It's important enough to me that I'm willing to release him from the expectation that he will do the job. Perhaps Stephen is clever enough to have devised a permanent way to escape washing dishes. But I think he's too tired right after dinner to think about dishes, and he'd rather tackle the job later. If I can't live with that, then I have a choice: I can do the work myself, or I can live with it being done on his terms. If I elect to do it myself, I owe it to him to do so without resentment.

Dividing Responsibilities with a Work-at-Home Spouse or Full-Time Caregiver

IN A marriage where both spouses work full-time, or close to it, the two generally have different expectations of each other than in a marriage where one spends most of his or her time at home. If this arrangement exists because a spouse is disabled or ill or has taken on the role of full-time homemaker, expectations are fairly clear. The disabled spouse may have few household responsibilities, and the full-time homemaker may willingly take on the whole job description. Conflict is more likely to arise when a spouse is home because he or she is taking care of kids part- or full-time or when he or she works from home.

I write a self-syndicated advice column on work and family issues called "Advice from A–Z," which appears in several East Coast daily newspapers. Here's what one work-from-home wife asked me:

> My business has been self-sustaining and profitable for more than eight years. I contribute equally to the household finances, which my husband and I share, even during my slow periods, since I bank my income in advance to support these downtimes.

When I experience the occasional downtime, my husband, who is otherwise highly supportive, seems to revert to a "well you are home all day doing nothing so you can do everything around the house" mode. It causes stress between us, as I view this behavior as a minor form of betrayal. While I remain busy trying to locate work and lessen my downtime, I receive an onslaught of requests to pick up dry cleaning, care for the lawn, and take on several other house-related projects he'd otherwise be responsible for and never even consider asking.

I used to happily run errands for him during these slower periods, until it became out of control. Every time I mentioned downtime, it seemed he'd mentally prepare a list of to-dos for me. I've now gotten to the point where I try not to mention when I've reached these periods, as it lessens my stress level. But I feel that's somewhat dishonest, and I wonder if there's a better solution. Any advice?

This is part of what I suggested:

For the time being, put aside any negative judgments and assumptions about your husband that fuel your anger. Maybe everything bad you are thinking about his motivations and attitude is correct. Or maybe it's entirely wrong, and your interpretation of his behavior is what is making you angry, not his actual behavior. As a temporary experiment, assume that he has only the most positive of intentions and that this is more a reflection of him than of you.

For example: Perhaps your husband is feeling down about himself and his inability to get things done at home because he's always working outside of the house. He's asking you to relieve his pressure, which he's reluctant to tell you directly because he interprets it as a failure on his part to be a productive caregiver and husband.

Maybe he sees both of you as a team, which is a positive statement of how he views your marriage, and he hopes that since the demands on each of you are so great, one person can pick up the slack when the other has downtime. If he had the opportunity to do the same for you, he would, but his career doesn't allow that.

Remember, men often judge productivity by concrete results, and to your husband, when you don't look busy, you aren't. He may not realize he's overloading you, because he doesn't understand what you are doing with your time when your business is slow.

Educate him—and not with a tone of voice that is defiant or angry. Instead, say, "I know that we're a team and that the items you are asking me to do have to get done by one of us. Let me tell you what I've got going on this week, how I'm using my time to increase my business, and when I have available time to do that. Let's make a plan together to get these tasks accomplished."

When you receive your husband's requests as if he were an arrogant, self-centered taskmaster ordering you to be his servant, you will always get angry. Try seeing him as an overwhelmed husband who doesn't know how to effectively ask for help, and then teach him how best to elicit your support.

Alison and George ran into conflict because George, a stay-at-home parent to their four children, was angry that his wife was working overtime and on weekends, forcing him to work overtime in his job as parent and housekeeper. Although he participated willingly and well in his "houseparent" role during certain defined hours, he was resentful of the extra hours he was required to be on duty. He wanted Alison to

U NFORTUNATELY, MANY of us operate from basic mind-sets that we are unerring observers of objective reality. We are unshakable in our certainty that what we see is indeed what has happened, and that what we hear is exactly what has been said. We will go to our graves arguing that we are right about our interpretation of events. To hear some of us in the heat of disagreement would lead to the conclusion that we are endowed with photographic memories, the acuity of eagles, the flawless objectivity of videocassettes, and the intuition of infallible psychics. The illusion of perfect perception which we so dogmatically uphold often turns out to be the very instrument of our relational demise.

—Eric Cohen, *You Owe Me*

come home and share some of the housework she was leaving to him all day long. Alison relates how she responded to ease the tension:

One day we were grousing about the chores and who should do what. The bulk of it was resting on George's shoulders, and he was right—it wasn't fair. I never once took out the trash. Perhaps it was my subconscious telling me that "only men" did that. I quickly turned that around. Just because he was home more than I was didn't mean I couldn't do laundry. I offered to help do the lawn, but he said he'd rather mow the lawn, since he had a particular way of doing it.

What finally resulted is that I joined the flex-schedule program at my work where I could have every other Monday off and still carry a full load, and I began to pitch in more around the house. Bingo—the concept of teamwork was born. Neither one of us likes to do dishes, so we do them together. He does laundry better than I do (believe it or not!), so he does the washing, and I do the folding. On the weekends, he gets a break from the kids, and we work together on any remaining chores.

Notice that if the previous paragraphs had been written with Alison and George's roles reversed, it would be almost expected. The guy comes home from work and doesn't pitch in to help his beleaguered wife. We aren't used to seeing the same situation through the eyes of a stay-at-home dad and a female executive who has so divorced herself from the responsibilities at home that she neglects to contribute much of anything except her paycheck.

Alison demonstrates how the responsibility is often on the parent who is *not* working from home to own responsibility for creating the problem and to do something about it. Too often that parent only gets defensive and rationalizes how hard he or she is working and why it's ridiculous to expect them to take out the garbage after a twelve-hour workday. The smart spouse, male or female, who works outside of the home knows that what is needed is an attitude adjustment to, "You're right; I need to be helping you more around the house. How can we make this work? What do you really need from me?"

Alison understood that this was an issue of *consideration*, not just of dividing the workload. Regardless of the complaints you and your spouse have about each other, both of you are looking for the same thing: respect. When one person acts as if her time is more precious and valuable than the other's, *the fight over who does what is really a fight about feeling valued in the relationship.*

Guaranteed, for every woman who is furious about what her husband isn't doing in the house, you'll find a guy who isn't doing what he needs to in the relationship. This is a guy who rarely says thank you or notices the dozens of details she handles throughout the day. He doesn't compliment her. She's not just angry about her workload burden; she's angry that her husband takes her for granted.

Mary was irate that her husband complained that she did not earn enough money in her home-based business while he also expected her to serve up dinner every night, but she found a way to help him understand:

> If he starts bitching about the lack of money coming in and how we're hurting because I haven't gotten paid lately, I remind him that he really enjoyed that potato-leek soup that I slaved over yesterday. I couldn't have made that if I'd been spinning out press releases all day! Likewise, if he starts complaining that a cleaning lady just isn't doing the laundry right, I'll remind him that thanks to the cleaning lady, I was able to pick up a new piece of business.
>
> One day I told him, "If you want fresh escarole with the sand removed from every leaf for supper on a day when I'm working, you will have to make it yourself." This did two things: It made him realize just how much work is involved in making that escarole dish, and it made him realize that the escarole couldn't be a priority on a day when both of us are working and we're dealing with the kids.

No household task is too insignificant to deserve gratitude. Expressing appreciation costs no money, and it can be done in ten seconds. Praising your spouse is a habit you can develop, a muscle that gets stronger with use. Although you may fantasize about a husband who happily takes on half of the household burden, I bet you'd settle agreeably for a third if he didn't assume that the other two-thirds were your job just because you are his wife and if he thanked you often for the work that you did.

Let Him Do What He's Good At, Instead of Insisting on Fifty-Fifty

STOP COUNTING how many hours your husband is spending on housework, and start paying more attention to what he's doing. Who cares if you are clocking more hours, as long as he's an involved, nonresentful partner willing to share the work. If you and your husband approach the problem with mutual respect, you can probably find a solution that works for both of you. Perhaps he will do the grocery shopping or the laundry, and you'll feed the dog and keep the kitchen clean. The task he does, especially if it's one you dread, may make your household responsibilities seem equitable.

> Remember, every person you meet is wearing a sign that says, "Make me feel important."
>
> —Mary Kay Ash, founder of Mary Kay Cosmetics

In our house, I cook every meal unless I'm out of town. I'm thinking about what's for dinner when I wake up, and it wouldn't be unusual for me to take something out of the freezer at breakfast time to prepare for dinner.

At the breakfast table, I might be looking at a recipe book to see whether we have all the ingredients in the house for a dish I'd like to make that evening. Doing this would never, ever occur to my husband. He doesn't start thinking about dinner until dinnertime. If he were cooking the meals, we'd have rice, noodles, tofu, and salad most nights. If he wanted to serve tofu with a sauce we didn't have, he'd go to the supermarket for it a half hour before he was going to start cooking, and if there were nothing for salad in the house, we'd skip it till he got around to the supermarket.

I often tell my husband, it's not the work of cooking the meals that grates on me sometimes; it's having to dream up dinner for a large family of diverse appetites every single day that is taxing. But I'm good at it, and Stephen isn't, so I do it; otherwise, I'd be eating a lot of tofu.

Instead of dividing household responsibilities according to how much time they take, measure the effort instead. One task that may be fairly effortless to you could be onerous to your spouse. One wife shared with me apologetically that her husband does all of the cooking, because she's a terrible cook and he enjoys it. He gets a lot of mileage out of doing that one job, especially because she feels guilty that she isn't fulfilling the "good wife" role by cooking her husband's meals.

If your spouse isn't doing his fair share, pick your top two or three most dreaded responsibilities and ask him if he'll do at least one of them, or maybe even all three. If you promise to leave him alone and stop complaining, that could be incentive enough for him to cooperate.

Taking Care of Your Husband Is Not Such a Bad Thing

SO, YOUR Prince Charming turned out to have some flaws. Before you fling all of the arrows, take a good, hard look at yourself. Do you think your husband is getting everything he ever wanted out of a wife? Anything missing in his fantasies? He probably has a few complaints about marriage, too, but before you get worked up over it, take a moment to ponder. Are there other ways that he takes care of you and the children? Are you missing his love for you because you're so darned mad at him that you can't appreciate (or even see) his good points anymore?

Maybe the best reason of all to do more than our fair share of the housework is that our husbands need us to, and taking care of our husbands is still a good thing, women's rights or not. I make my husband homemade bagels and granola every week, not because I have to but because he loves my homemade bagels, and granola out of the supermarket box is outrageously expensive. It's a perk he gets by being married to me, just the way I appreciate that he can fix anything that is fixable on this planet.

My husband would totally understand if I told him that because I'm a busy working woman, the homemade bagels and granola have to go. But with a minimum of effort, I start my husband's day off with a clear message: "I value you enough to take the time to serve you."

I use the words "serve you" with no apologies. We working wives have become so consumed with equal rights, equal partnership, entitlements, and making sure that we have our

M Y HUSBAND was diagnosed with cancer three years ago. He needed me. I needed him to need me. Normally he's the one who's in control of everything. But now he wanted to lay his head on my shoulder. He gave me a responsibility, and it made me feel very powerful and very strong.

—Celine Dion, entertainer

independence that we have lost the art of serving our partners, just as we often hope they would serve us.

Vicki describes beautifully the struggle she had with reconciling dual parts of herself—the woman who wanted to take care of her husband, and the woman who was damned if she'd ever let herself be considered his maid:

When my children were small, I was a stay-at-home mom. My husband was in construction, so I dutifully got up every morning and made him a lunch with the typical boring sandwich, fruit, and cookies. Day after day, year after year, for eight years, I made his lunches.

Then, when both of my kids were in school, I went back to work. I got up every morning and made my lunch but drew the line about making my husband's lunch. As a result, he bought lunch from lunch wagons or convenience stores for the next sixteen or seventeen years.

He is a strong-willed Italian, and I am a strong-willed Irish woman. I felt I would be letting him control me if I made his lunch. For years, I carried around this "lunch chip" on my shoulder.

One day, my husband was working out on a job with no lunch facilities. He decided to make his own lunch, which included only a couple of pieces of fruit—not much of a lunch. Something clicked, and I took the chip off my shoulder, looked at it, and threw it away. I decided to make my husband's lunch because I chose to, not because I had to.

This change of attitude affected other areas as well. I no longer had to be defensive about everything my husband said, and our relationship became more relaxed. We would go out to breakfast or lunch just to be together. I rediscovered that after thirty-two years of marriage, my husband still made me laugh and that we could almost finish each other's sentences. When I flipped that old defensive chip off my shoulder, a weight was lifted from me, showing me a world full of possibilities.

Balance Your Desire to Be the "Good Wife" with Drawing the Line When You Need To

IT IS good sometimes to please our husbands and let go of the worship of equity. Sometimes, though, you can take this idea too far and crave your husband's approval and acknowledgment of "good wife" status too much, to the point where you betray your own best interests. This is an artful dance we are mastering, and all of us are clumsy at times, tripping over ourselves even when we know better. I'll share a simple example.

It was a typical Friday morning in our household. I had gotten our three young children dressed for school, made their breakfast and their school lunches, and started preparing fresh challah (bread) for that night's Sabbath dinner. The weekly cleaning service was coming at 11 A.M. (my one concession that I can't do it all), so I started straightening the kitchen before their arrival. Meanwhile, my then working-at-home husband went jogging, ate his breakfast, and read the newspaper. I got the kids off to school, did some banking, checked e-mail for my home-based business, and finished the next step of bread preparation, and before I knew it, it was 9:35.

My weekly women's study class, five minutes away, started at 9:30. I shouted out to my husband that I was late for class and was scooting out the door. He made a simple comment: "Are you going to clean up the clutter in the house before the cleaning people come?"

This ritual takes about half an hour. It usually involves picking the kids' dirty laundry up off the floor so that the vacuum will find the rug and putting away the mishmash of kid belongings that get in the way of the cleaning service. If I went to my women's class, the cleaners would already be engaged in their work by the time I returned.

My husband's words might have been a simple inquiry: "Are you going to do this, or should I?" But I *heard* a different message: "How is the house going to get picked up before the cleaning people get here? You should have done it before you left for class!"

I needed my husband to notice that I had been working all morning to take care of the family's needs. I wanted him to say cheerfully as I rushed out the door to class, "I know you've been working hard all morning and didn't have time to pick up the clutter in the house. I'll take care of it." I would have hugged him and felt like we were on the same team.

But that's not what happened.

I was furious with his question. I told him so. I announced that it would have been nice if he had just taken care of the chore instead of implying that I was wrong for not doing it. He protested that he was only asking me a question. This infuriated me even more. Couldn't he at least be honest with me, and with himself?

I discovered that morning that I was willing to pay a high price in order to be a "good wife" in my husband's eyes. Too high a price.

Despite the voice in my head that shouted, "No, don't do that!" I skipped my class and toiled away for the next hour on household chores. I stewed about not being appreciated and about my husband's self-centered behavior. I talked myself into a total funk and felt distant from my husband for days.

Ever since that day, I've paid closer attention to the times I give away too much of myself in order to win my husband's approval—and resent it later. Now that my husband is no longer working from home (he has since begun new employment outside of the home), the responsibility falls squarely back on my shoulders to de-clutter the house for the cleaners, and that's okay. At least we're clear about it.

I am strongly in favor of serving our husbands with love and respect. But stop short of giving up something you really need because you don't have the courage to tolerate a bit of tension with your husband. You won't always win your husband's love and approval, no matter how "good" you are, so sometimes, in order to take care of yourself, you'll have to live with Mr. Grumpy until he gets over it.

> When a man does work around the house, he's doing us a favor. When she does it, it's her duty.
>
> —Laura Doyle,
> *The Surrendered Wife*

From Fantasy to Reality: Ways to Get His Help Without Ordering Him Around

LET'S EMPLOY the serenity prayer: May you find the serenity to accept your husband's inequities in the household responsibilities department and to tolerate his stubbornness, and, all the while, may you subtly inspire him to give more!

Here are some simple ideas for turning your mate into a willing partner, instead of a resentful hostage:

- Marriage is not just about getting what you want. Your husband, too, has wants, needs, and desires, and after having read this far, you probably have a pretty good idea of what they are. Maybe you've got it all backward. You may be waiting for him to help you more first so that you'll become interested in sex again or feel inspired to do more in the kitchen than warming frozen chicken nuggets. Consider this: If you are an attentive lover, help him in his business if he asks, and occasionally serve him a favorite dish—he just might lend a more willing helping hand.

- Don't apologize all the time. Apologies are a particularly gruesome female habit. Ever notice how we say "I'm sorry" when we have nothing to be sorry for? If you don't have time to do something and it isn't exclusively your job, don't apologize for not being able to do it—unless you are breaking a clear contract you made with your husband.

- Let your husband know when you need his help. If he's perfectly capable of doing it, ask for his help without feeling guilty. Don't overcompensate for your guilt by yelling at him. Just be calm and clear about what you need.

■ Don't wait until you are exhausted and then explode and dump a list of demands on your husband, all of them needed by yesterday. Ask for help before you reach the point of exhaustion.

■ Did I mention sex? Oh, yes, try a bit more sex. In some men, it does wonders to inspire the willingness to clean the bathroom tub or to more easily agree that you need paid help.

■ If you want your husband to help, be very specific with him. Don't say, "This house is a mess, and I want you to help me clean it up more often!" He hasn't a clue what you are talking about. What does "clean up the house" mean to you, and to him?

■ Ask for what you want (instead of complaining about what you don't want). Tell him clearly but without the condescending voice. Spell it out so there isn't any ambiguity.

■ Compliment and thank him—no matter how insignificant the job or how entitled you feel. Don't you appreciate his gratitude when you do something for him?

What you give out will come back to you. Say thank you more often, and you will have more reasons to say thank you. Look at your husband through the lens of appreciation, instead of resentment, and your stress level will lower—before he even picks up a dish towel.

CHAPTER NINE

Conclusion

Taking Stock and Keeping Perspective

N OW THAT you have reached the end of this book, you should have a different state of mind regarding the challenge of gaining your husband's permission to prosper than you did before you began reading. It is my hope that you are well on your way to creating the goodwill-centered marriage described in chapter 1. I hope that all of the following statements resonate with you as truth:

1. You have lost any shame or reluctance to acknowledge your craving for your husband's approval and blessings for your continued and growing prosperity. You understand that a wife's attachment to her husband as her partner in the deepest sense, in and out of work, is the engine that drives her in her life. It is not noble to work on independence from him, rather than dependence; it is counterproductive. A working wife is far more prosperous and self-confident when she is in sync with her husband than when she is pulling away from him. I hope that you are *interdependent* with your husband,

needing him as much as he needs you, and that you're fine with that, because that's what a loving, committed union is all about.

2. You understand that permission to prosper does not happen in one moment in time, nor do you lose it that way. It's an attitude that ebbs and flows throughout your married life. You may be married to a man who graces you with it more often during certain periods of your life together than at other times. You are learning not to give up on him if he's particularly triggered right now by a change in you or your career or needs of his own that aren't being met. You are also more hopeful that at any point the two of you could find a new way of relating to each other that will be more satisfying to both of you. You aren't so pessimistic that you think you have to live with whatever faults you see in him, because now, more than ever, you understand how far-reaching can be your impact on changing him and the way you relate.

3. You accept that you will probably never achieve nirvana—marriage to the ideal man, who epitomizes the perfect partner at your side to emotionally, spiritually, and physically support you in every way you need, at any moment you need it. You are learning to give your husband a break, to forgive him his foibles, and to appreciate him in new ways. You understand that the more you do for him, the more love he will probably give you. You are less focused than you were at the beginning of this book on what you aren't *getting* from him and more focused on what you need to *give* in order to create the mutually loving relationship that fulfills you.

4. Even if you purchased this book hoping to learn how to change your man—and you just might do so—you also have learned that much of the permission-to-prosper issue resides within you, in lowering your unrealistic ideals, in working on your own internal blocks and fears that prohibit your success, and on not allowing you to use your husband as a convenient scapegoat for all of your career disappointments. You are also learning to live with the uneasy feeling that comes from marriage to a man who doesn't always approve of your actions. As much as you crave his permission, you are also learning that you don't have to give up core needs of your own in order to gain his approval. Sometimes, you'll make the decision to put yourself first, but you can do so with love and respect.

As I hope the previous statements resonate positively with you, I also hope the following joke, although humorous, does not resonate truthfully with you at all:

A woman accompanies her husband to the doctor's office. After his checkup, the doctor calls the wife into his office alone. He says, "Your husband is suffering from a very severe stress disorder. If you don't do the following, your husband will surely deteriorate and die.

"Each morning," the doctor instructs, "fix him a healthy breakfast. Be pleasant at all times. For lunch make him a nutritious meal. For dinner prepare an especially nice meal for him. Have the dinner waiting for him on the table, hot, as he arrives home from work. Don't burden him with chores. Don't discuss your problems with him; it will only make his stress worse. No nagging is allowed. You must also compliment him at least five or six times a day, telling him how brilliant and talented he is. And most important, never disagree with him.

"If you can do this for the next ten months to a year," the doctor says, "I think your husband will regain his health completely."

On the way home, the husband asks his wife, "What did the doctor say?"

She replies, "He said you're going to die."

Even though it might be increasingly unfashionable these days to take good care of your man, I hope that you do so unapologetically, with gratitude and full dedication of your heart, in whatever available time you can create with each other. In exchange, you will be amply rewarded with the love and support you have always craved in a marriage partnership.

What Kind of Marriage Are You Creating?

MARRIAGES ARE always works in progress, as we are. You probably purchased this book because there was tension in your career, your marriage, or both. The older I get and the longer I am married, the more I see how a marriage is a living entity that evolves over time, growing either stronger or weaker, depending on how you take care of it. Whatever notion I might have had as a young child about a fairy-tale, happily-ever-after life with my husband has been replaced by a slightly more cynical, and definitely more realistic, view of what a marriage is and can be.

I have grieved the loss of the dream of unconditional love— the enchanting idea that somewhere in the world is a person who will love me no matter what I do, always and forever. We enter

M Y HUSBAND told me something early on in our relationship that set the basis for our relationship. He said, "Home is where we come for love, support, and anything that we need. The outside world is where we have our battles, not at home." He asked me to leave the negative emotions of my work problems outside, and he assured me that together, we could solve anything.

—Kathy

the world as infants, receiving that kind of love from our parents. But then, as we grow up and individualize, our parents often fail to give us unconditional love, even though they might profess to. Unconditional love with no judgments, no strings attached, can't exist in any human relationship—only a divine one.

We enter into marriage hoping to receive unconditional love, and we bang up against the same wall—we are married to a human being, with his or her own agenda, ego, needs, and preferences. Loving our spouses unconditionally is a struggle, too, because there's just so much about them that is frustrating and needs changing.

Married love doesn't always feel good. It sometimes hurts—a lot. Married love can be lonely, frustrating, and boring, and there is probably no one on earth who can make you angrier than can your husband. And yet, at the end of the day, it is possible that together you are creating a thing of beauty, even if it isn't perfect.

Marriage evolves as you and your husband grow and mature. What kind of marriage are you creating? Is your heart filled with gratitude or resentment? Do you feel loved and cherished in a fundamental way, and are you communicating the same to your life partner? Does your mate know how much you love him and need him, or have you been spending too much time lately complaining about how he's letting you down? How much time do you spend contemplating how you can serve him, rather than dwelling on how you can manipulate him into giving you what you need? Are you collaborative partners with a common vision or opponents concerned about getting out of each other's way?

How is your career working for you and your spouse? Is it the elephant in the room that no one wants to talk about, or is it a blessing each of you speaks of with thankfulness? Does working make you happier, more purposeful, and more generous? Is prosperity flowing into your life the way you'd like? If not, do you know where you are blocked? The privilege of being a human being is that, at any time, you can change your life. We are not prisoners.

If your work is turning you into a woman, a wife, and a mother whom you do not respect or like very much, I hope that you will find the courage to modify your career. The years fly by; the money comes and goes. What truly remains at the end of our time in this universe are the relationships we've created and any way we've made this earth a better place than before we were born.

When was the last time you and your spouse really laughed, at yourselves, with each other, at life? Take your marriage and your career seriously, but never forget that we are all a speck in the universe, and our entire lifetimes are over in the blink of an eye. So much of what we get worked up about just doesn't matter. Too much of what really does matter isn't getting our attention.

Although it's important to let go of unrealistic notions of unconditional love in every moment of your marriage, it's important to hold to a vision of union with your husband that is deeper than any other adult relationship you can experience. Rebetzin Jungries, author of *The Committed Life,* conveys a beautiful image to remember:

> Even as Adam and Eve were one entity that God split into two, so every husband and wife were originally one soul. Upon entering this world, they are split, but they become reunited through marriage. Human beings, different from animals who have no desire for oneness outside of procreation, yearn to find completion through connecting with their soul mates, their other halves.
>
> This need is an innate desire embedded in our souls, and it is only because of our cultural biases that we distrust this natural instinct. We are taught to safeguard our independence zealously, to look with suspicion at any request as a form of manipulation, and to regard giving as "being had."
>
> Under such circumstances, the demands of marriage—giving, sharing—become burdensome and are offered only grudgingly. If you love your spouse as yourself, you will never feel put upon, because if it's good for your mate, it's good for you as well.

Who Is Packing Your Parachute?

I CLOSE this chapter, and this book, with one final story with a powerful lesson.

Captain Charles Plumb was a jet fighter pilot in Vietnam who was shot down and parachuted into enemy hands. He spent six years in a Communist prison, and now he is a motivational speaker, teaching his audiences the lessons he learned from that ordeal.

As Plumb tells the story, many years after his capture and release, he and his wife were sitting in a restaurant when a man approached, announcing himself as the sailor who had packed the captain's parachute the day his aircraft was shot down. That man saved Plumb's life, since the parachute kept him from sure death. His fate was determined by a sailor who had spent hours weaving and folding his parachute. Who knew at the time that Plumb's life would depend on this sailor's fastidious work?

Plumb asks his audience, "Who's packing your parachute?"

Too often in dual-career households, each spouse packs his own parachute. You occupy a house together but don't act as if your life depended on each other's support.

How would you treat your husband if you knew that his life depended on you? If you knew that the parachute you were packing for him could mean the difference between his living and dying, would you pack it any differently? Have you allowed your husband to pack your parachute, or have you insisted on doing it yourself?

Go fight the big fights; soar like an eagle into a prosperous, rewarding career. But never forget that you don't have to do this alone when you are married. You have a parachute to protect you and to give you a soft space to fall should you run into turbulence or get shot down by the enemy. The man you married can help you stay safe.

Let him know that you might have to leave him from time to time, to go fly as you must to accomplish your mission. Also, be sure he knows that the parachute you carry with you—filled with his love and support—keeps you flying with confidence, and even if you are never in true danger, it comforts you to know that it is there just in case.

Let your husband know that when you are done flying, you look forward with joy to returning home to him. Your husband can watch you soar with greater ease if he knows that he packed your parachute and that you still need him when your plane lands.

L ET'S CONTINUE the dialogue. Converse with me about what it means to prosper in a marriage. E-mail me at az@azriela.com or azriela@mindspring.com, or visit my Web site (www.permissiontoprosper.com or www.azriela.com), where you can sign up for free e-mail newsletters to assist you in your career and your marriage.

Bibliography

Since I have been writing about marriage for the past several years, I am often asked for my recommendation for "good books to read besides yours." All of the following books helped inform my thinking on the topic of permission to prosper. Those marked with an asterisk (*) are the top ten books that I consider required reading for any couple committed to creating the best marriage possible. Each of these books has helped me enormously in my own marriage, and each is still, to my knowledge, available in print. I'm delighted to pass the gift along.

*Christensen, Andrew, and Neil S. Jacobson. *Reconcilable Differences*. New York: The Guilford Press, 2000.

*Cohen, Eric J., and Gregory Sterling. *You Owe Me: The Emotional Debts That Cripple Relationships*. Far Hills, N.J.: New Horizon Press, 1999.

*Doherty, William J. *Take Back Your Marriage: Sticking Together in a World That Pulls Us Apart*. New York: The Guilford Press, 2001.

Doyle, Laura. *The Surrendered Wife: A Practical Guide to Finding Intimacy, Passion, and Peace with Your Man*. New York: Simon and Schuster, 1999.

Evans, Patricia. *Controlling People: How to Recognize, Understand, and Deal with People Who Try to Control You.* Avon, Mass.: Adams Media Corporation, 2000.

Farrell, Warren. *Why Men Are the Way They Are.* New York: Berkeley Books, 1986.

Fisher, Bruce, and Nina Hart. *Loving Choices: An Experience in Growing Relationships.* Atascadero, Calif.: Impact Publishers.

*Gray, John. *Men Are from Mars, Women Are from Venus: A Practical Guide for Improving Communication and Getting What You Want in Your Relationships.* New York: HarperCollins, 1992.

Hartley, Fred. *Men and Marriage: What It Really Means to Keep That Promise.* Minneapolis: Bethany House Publishers, 1994.

Hochschild, Arlie. *The Second Shift.* New York: Avon, 1989, 1997.

Jaffe, Azriela. *Create Your Own Luck: 8 Principles of Attracting Good Fortune in Life, Love, and Work.* Holbrook, Mass.: Adams Media, 2000.

Jaffe, Azriela. *Honey, I Want to Start My Own Business: A Planning Guide for Couples.* New York: HarperBusiness, 1996.

Jaffe, Azriela. *Two Jews Can Still Be a Mixed Marriage: Reconciling Differences Over Judaism in Your Marriage.* New York: New Page Books, 2000.

*Jungreis, Rebbetzin Esther. *The Committed Life: Principles for Good Living from Our Timeless Past.* New York: Cliff Street Books, 1998.

Kingma, Daphne Rose. *The Men We Never Knew: How to Deepen Your Relationship with the Man You Love*. Berkeley, Calif.: Conari Press, 1994.

Markman, Howard J., Scott M. Stanley, and Susan L. Blumberg. *Fighting for Your Marriage: Positive Steps for Preventing Divorce and Preserving a Lasting Love*. San Francisco: Jossey-Bass, 1994.

Maushart, Susan. *Wifework: What Marriage Really Means for Women*. New York: Bloomsbury, 2001.

Mellan, Olivia, and Sherry Christie. *Money Shy to Money Sure: A Woman's Road Map to Financial Well Being*. New York: Walker and Company, 2001.

Minetor, Randi. *Breadwinner Wives and the Men They Marry: How to Have a Successful Marriage While Outearning Your Husband*. Far Hills, N.J.: New Horizon Press, 2002.

Notarius, Clifford I., and Howard J. Markman. *We Can Work It Out: How to Solve Conflicts, Save Your Marriage, and Strengthen Your Love for Each Other*. New York: Putnam, 1993.

Obsatz, Michael. *From Stalemate to Soulmate: A Guide to Mature, Committed, Loving Relationships*. Minneapolis: Augsburg Fortress, 1997.

O'Hanlon, Bill. *Do One Thing Different: Ten Simple Ways to Change Your Life*. New York: William Morrow and Company, 1999.

Orenstein, Peggy. *Flux: Women on Sex, Work, Love, Kids, and Life in a Half-Changed World*. New York: First Anchor Books, 2000.

*Page, Susan. *How One of You Can Bring the Two of You Together: Breakthrough Strategies to Resolve Your Conflicts and Reignite Your Love.* New York: Broadway Books, 1997.

Page, Susan. *If We're So in Love, Why Aren't We Happy? Using Spiritual Principles to Solve Real Problems and Restore Your Passion.* New York: Harmony Books, 2002.

*Page, Susan. *Now That I'm Married, Why Isn't Everything Perfect? The 8 Essential Traits of Couples Who Thrive.* New York: Little Brown and Company, 1994.

Phelps, Stanlee, and Nancy K. Austin. *The Assertive Woman.* Atascadero, Calif.: Impact Publishers, 2000.

Pransky, George S. *Divorce Is Not the Answer: A Change of Heart Will Save Your Marriage.* New York: TAB Books, McGraw-Hill, 1990.

Schwartz, Daylle Deanna. *All Men Are Jerks: Until Proven Otherwise.* Holbrook, Mass.: Adams Media, 1998.

Schwebel, Robert. *Who's on Top, Who's on Bottom: How Couples Can Learn to Share Power.* New York: New-Market Press, 1994.

Sterling, A. Justin. *What Really Works with Men: Solve 95% of Your Relationship Problems.* New York: Warner Books, 1992.

St. John, Noah. *Permission to Succeed: Unlocking the Mystery of Success Anorexia.* Dearfield Beach, Fla.: Health Communications, 1999.

Tessina, Tina B. *How to Be a Couple and Still Be Free.* North Hollywood, Calif.: New Castle Publishing, 1987, 2002.

Wallin, Pauline. *Taming Your Inner Brat: A Guide for Transforming Self-Defeating Behavior.* Hillsboro, Ore.: Beyond Words Publishing, 2001.

Warner, Jim. *Aspirations of Greatness: Mapping the Midlife Leader's Reconnection to Self and Soul.* New York: John Wiley and Sons, 2002.

★Weiner-Davis, Michele. *Divorce Busting: A Revolutionary and Rapid Program for Staying Together.* New York: Fireside, 1993.

★Weiner-Davis, Michele. *The Divorce Remedy: The Proven 7-Step Program for Saving Your Marriage.* New York: Simon and Schuster, 2001.

★Weiner-Davis, Michele. *A Woman's Guide to Changing Her Man: Without His Even Knowing It.* New York: Golden Books, 1998.

Wilson Solovic, Susan. *The Girl's Guide to Power and Success.* New York: Amacom, 2001.

Index

About the Author

Azriela Jaffe is the author of ten nonfiction books and is currently at work on her first novel on the theme of spiritual destiny in a marriage and family. Her recent books include *Create Your Own Luck: Eight Strategies to Attract Good Fortune into Your Life, Love, and Work; Two Jews Can Still Be a Mixed Marriage: Reconciling Differences Regarding Judaism in Your Marriage; Let's Go into Business Together: Eight Secrets to Successful Business Partnering;* and *Starting from No: Ten Strategies to Overcome Your Fear of Rejection and Succeed in Business.*

Azriela is also a nationally syndicated newspaper columnist, offering business advice to small business owners and their families. She is a widely quoted authority on small business relationships and work/family issues. Her work has been translated into several different languages, and she publishes two e-zines for more than 7,000 subscribers around the globe. She resides in Yardley, Pennsylvania, with her husband, Stephen, three children, and a teenage exchange student from Japan.